C000178548

HE DOVE 'N' KETCHED IT!

The Story of Melbourne Town Cricket Club 1861 to 2011

By Andrew C Heafield

First published in Great Britain 2011 by:
The Magic Attic Archives
c/o Sharpes Pottery Museum
West Street, Swadlincote
Derbyshire DE11 9DG

"HE DOVE 'N' KETCHED IT!"
The Story of Melbourne Town Cricket Club
1861 to 2011

Copyright © 2011 Andrew C Heafield

We acknowledge the support of Derbyshire County Council in the publication of this book.

Cover, design and book layout by The Magic Attic Archives

ISBN 978-0-9567861-0-4

DEDICATION

"When an old cricketer leaves the crease"

How many people who play for and against Melbourne Town Cricket Club (MTCC) at our current ground realise that they are treading in the footsteps of well over a thousand local cricketers who have appeared for the club over the past 150 years? From those Victorian origins to the present day, cricket has had a central place in the sporting fabric of the town.

Some very famous cricketers have appeared at the ground including Derbyshire Captains, England players and Captains of the Marylebone Cricket Club (MCC). The club, in 1875, even employed a professional cricketer, a Mr C Randon. Some Melbourne born cricketers have gone on to play county cricket; another had the distinction of, in 1902, playing against probably the world's most famous cricketer, Dr W G Grace. In 1966, R E J (Bob) Chambers opened the batting for Cambridge University side against the touring West Indies side which contained Gary Sobers and Wes Hall. The following season, in quite a contrast, he played for Melbourne.

However, only one cricketer, Jim Horsley, is on record as actually playing for Melbourne Town Cricket Club before going on to play County cricket for many years. In 1914 in the county championship match between Derbyshire and Leicestershire, Jim batted with the splendidly named, and Melbourne born, Norton Montressor Hughes-Hallett.

In the 1950s crowds of over one thousand came to watch testimonial matches held at the ground. People still come to watch, although in fewer numbers, but the intensity of the cricket played is still the same and, we hope, in a similar sporting manner to that of our cricketing ancestors.

This book doesn't set out to be a complete history of the club but has been pieced together from the memories of those cricketers still with us and the archives that exist. Inevitably with local cricket, where in most cases few records exist, a book such as this will raise debate as to the exact dates and happenings, particularly in a sport where two players can have a totally different memory of the same event, which can happen a day or a week after a match, especially if beer consumption has taken place! The book is also interspersed with advice and anecdotes on local cricket which should have relevance to cricketers of all abilities.

This book is dedicated to all Melbourne cricketers, with the words of Roy Harper, from "When an old cricketer leaves the crease".

"When the moment comes and the gathering stands
and the clock turns back to reflect,
on the years of grace as those footsteps trace
for the last time out of the act.
Well this way of life's recollection,
the hallowed strip in the haze,
the fabled men and the noonday sun
are much more than just yarns of their days."

Local cricket is there to be enjoyed for what it is and without undue analysis, no more and no less - very much like this publication.

Front Cover Photos

Top Left:	Les Jackson, George Ensor. A E Rhodes Testimonial Match, July 6th 1952
Top Right:	MTCC 1907
Bottom Left:	MTCC 2nd XI, 2010 Harry Lund Cup Final
Bottom Right:	Jim Horsley

CONTENTS

FOREWORD BY LORD RALPH KERR

"Many congratulations to the club on their 150th anniversary!"

It is with particular pleasure that I am writing the foreword to this book.

The Melbourne Town Cricket Club has always been highly thought of in my family and is a part of the rich tradition of clubs in Melbourne that form such an important fabric of our existence.

On attending the 2010 Legends of Cricket match to present the Lothian Trophy, named in honour of my great-grandfather I made a small speech on congratulating the winning Captain. I make no apologies on recalling it now as it sums up precisely what my family feel:

"Firstly can I say how honoured we feel that there is a trophy named in honour of our family in commemoration of the gift of the land by my great-grandfather to the people of Melbourne for sport and recreation. He would, I think, have been delighted that the cricket club has used the ground since then, as are we."

Many congratulations to the club on their 150th anniversary! I know they have many grand events planned to celebrate this magnificent occasion. I sincerely hope you will be able to attend them.

This book is a worthy addition to the many books on Melbourne and I hope that you enjoy reading it.

Lord Ralph Kerr
Melbourne Hall
Patron of the Melbourne Town Cricket Club.

Congratulations from Melbourne, Australia

MELBOURNE CRICKET CLUB

From the office of Stephen Gough Chief Executive Officer

15 November 2010

Lord Ralph Kerr,
Patron,
MELBOURNE TOWN CRICKET CLUB

Dear Lord Ralph,

It is with great pleasure that I write to you today, the 172nd Anniversary of the foundation of the Melbourne Cricket Club in Victoria, Australia, to pass on to our colleagues at the Melbourne Cricket Club in Derbyshire, England, our committee and members' hearty congratulations for your own club's 150th Anniversary year in 2011.

Our Club was established during the infancy of settlement in the Port Phillip district by a small band of colonists seeking to recreate some of the traditions and customs from the homeland at a time where cricket was growing into a key recreational pursuit across society. While they transplanted a little bit of English culture here, over the years it has grown and developed into a distinctly Australian sporting institution with over 100,000 members and a ground with a rich history including hosting the first Test and One-Day International matches.

Cricket continues to link our two nations, where the love for the great game remains a common part of our culture. Nowhere is this more evident than during an Ashes series. As I write we are working on final preparations for the England tour of the summer of 2010/2011 highlighted by our traditional Test match commencing on Boxing Day. While there will be a strong rivalry on the field, off it we very much look forward to renewing old friendships and making new ones with our visitors, as the social side of the game is one of its pleasures.

Once again I offer congratulations to your club and wish you all the best for your 150th anniversary season.

Yours sincerely,

STEPHEN GOUGH
Chief Executive Officer

MCG PO Box 175 East Melbourne Vic 8002 Australia T 61 3 9657 8811   F 61 3 9650 6768 www.mcc.org.au www.mcg.org.au

Congratulations from Melbourne, Australia

The Rt. Hon. The Lord Mayor of Melbourne

April 2011

Lord Ralph Kerr
Patron
Melbourne Town Cricket Club

My Lord

It is a privilege to congratulate you on the Melbourne Town Cricket Club's 150th anniversary. My city is named in honour of the Viscount Melbourne and is the home of the greatest cricket ground in the world, the MCG!

150 years ago was an interesting time in Melbourne Australia. We were at the peak of the Victorian gold rush and the influx of people led to massive growth and prosperity. For a time Melbourne was the second largest city in the Empire after London.

To the Cricket Club in the original "Melbourne" congratulations on your longevity. It is my hope that your club continues to produce great cricketers.

But not too great.

Yours faithfully, *warm personal regards*

Robert Doyle

Robert Doyle
Lord Mayor

City of Melbourne
PO Box 1603 Melbourne
Victoria 3001 Australia

Telephone 613 9658 9825
Facsimile 61 3 9654 2628

INTRODUCTION

"For when the One Great Scorer comes to mark against your name"

In the 150 years of Melbourne cricket it's no surprise that many players have represented the club with distinction for a great number of years and some are still continuing to do so. It's estimated that well over 1,000 different players have turned out for the club during that period.

Looking not so far back, current Club Chairman, Terence (Tel) Potts, first played for the club as a twelve year old in 1960 and still turns out for the occasional game. Colin Wakefield has played for the club since 1967: he still topped the 2nd XI bowling averages in 2010 and is looking forward to playing in 2011. Allowing for playing 25 games a year, that means 'Wakie' has played over 1,000 games for the club. Mike Starkie has played since the 1970s and John Hallifield has appeared in each of the past 45 seasons and is determined to make it to the fifty mark and beyond.

Looking at the past generations, Harold Hodgkinson, a club stalwart for many years, first played for the club in 1927 and was still doing so in the late 1960s. The Andrews family had a 70 year connection with the club that went from the early 1900s. Roy Grummett and Stan and Richard Hatton were other club stalwarts who first made their mark in the 1950s and continued to play well into the 1980s. Lennie Barber played in the 1950s and still serves the club as assistant groundsman. Even in these modern times, there is no doubt that some of the current Melbourne cricketers will carry on the tradition of a long playing career and service to the club. Current first team Captain Alex Slater has played since 1988 and is still a relative youngster.

That's not to say that the club is forever wallowing in nostalgia and hankering for past times; these are exciting days for the club with the setting up of kwik cricket sessions, age group teams and new coaches being trained. The aim is to produce young local players who will come through the ranks and take the club onwards and upwards.

Lifelong friendships have been forged, deaths mourned, wives met, children born and generations have played with the next generation at the club.

Not everyone who has played for the club has been a great sportsman, but to think that they should be is missing the point; they've all been treated as though they were. Although talking about American football, American writer Grantland Rice could easily have been talking about Melbourne cricket when he said:

"For when the One Great Scorer comes
To mark against your name,
He marks - not that you won or lost -
But how you played the Game."

TOWN HISTORY

"If God made a better place, he kept it to himself."

Melbourne is a small, Georgian market town in South Derbyshire, England. It is about eight miles south of Derby and two miles from the River Trent. In 1837 a then tiny settlement in Australia was named after William Lamb, 2nd Viscount Melbourne, Queen Victoria's first Prime Minister, and thus indirectly takes its name from Melbourne Hall, seat of the Lamb family, and the town of Melbourne, Derbyshire.

There is much debate on whether Melbourne is a town or a village; certainly with a population of around 4,500, it is a small town but then compare the two definitions:

1. A village in the UK is a compact settlement of houses, smaller in size than a town, and generally based on agriculture or, in some areas, mining, quarrying or sea fishing.
2. A town traditionally was a settlement which had a charter to hold a market or fair and therefore became a "market town". Market towns were distinguished from villages in that they were the economic hub of a surrounding area, and were usually larger and had more facilities.

Both descriptions could easily fit, but for most inhabitants it is a large village, which makes even more confusing the fact that the cricket club has been Melbourne Town Cricket Club since its inception. Similarly confusing for this book, Melbourne is referred to as both.

The name Melbourne means 'mill stream'. It was first recorded in the Domesday Book (DB 1086 Mileburne = mill stream) as a royal manor. The town has approximately 4,500 inhabitants and in the past been known chiefly for its market gardens, shoe manufacture and textiles, though other small industries exist and it has an industrial estate.

Between the wars there were about sixty growers of fruit and vegetables in Melbourne. By 1980 this number had fallen to around twenty. Now only a handful are in the business.

The 2001 census counted 4,599 inhabitants in Melbourne compared to an estimated 3,500 in 1861. One major change has been the travel to work habits of the population; nowadays it is estimated that 80% of the population travel to work compared with roughly the same figure who worked locally 150 years ago.

The vast majority of Melbourne residents in 1861 would have worked locally; the census of the time reveals that the most popular occupations were agricultural labourers, boot and shoe makers and domestic servants.

Melbourne has several churches, chapels, an infant and junior school, shops, pubs and a large hall (formerly The Rectory) with important formal gardens and the former mill pool alongside. The church of St Michael with St Mary is probably on the site of a much earlier Anglo-Saxon building, and is regarded as one of the finest Norman parish churches in the country. It is mostly 12th century, with some later additions. It was built as a retreat for the Bishops of Carlisle, who were under constant threat of raids and violence in their northern diocese. The church possesses a two tower facade, unique amongst Norman parish churches, a crossing tower, a nave of five bays, aisles and transepts. All of this is Norman with the exception of the 17th century aisle and east windows. The south transept contains alabaster slabs to Henry Hardie, who died in 1613, Anne Harding, who died in 1673 and Sir Robert Harding, who died in 1679.

Melbourne once had its own castle, a large structure with many towers. It was dismantled in the early 17th century after falling into disrepair, and now only a single wall stands behind Castle House, a partly 17th century brick construction. John, Duke of Bourbon, who was the most important prisoner taken at Agincourt in 1415, was detained in the castle for nineteen years. It was also considered as a place of detention for Mary, Queen of Scots in 1583 but too many adaptations were required and the plan was abandoned.

Melbourne Hall is open to the public during the month of August. It was built as a rectory for the Bishops of Carlisle who leased it to Sir John Coke in 1628. His great grandson acquired the freehold and subsequent generations of the family have altered and enlarged the hall and gardens. The current residents are Lord and Lady Ralph Kerr, son and daughter-in-law of the 12th Marquis of Lothian. The gardens contain a wonderfully ornate wrought iron arbour, built by Robert Bakewell, and known locally as 'The Birdcage'. Robert Bakewell, the country's most famous wrought iron smith lived in Melbourne for a time in what was then called the Stone House. More recently it has been known as Tythe Barn Cottage but reverted to its old name in the 1980s.

A panoramic view of Melbourne Market Place
Original watercolour by Jayne Wright (4)

Melbourne has a strong musical tradition with a highly esteemed operatic society specialising in Gilbert and Sullivan operas as well as a male voice choir which has performed internationally. The Melbourne Town Band was re-formed in 1993 and is highly popular. Its conductor, Brendan O'Neill has just started another musical venture, Bon Jazz, a twenty one piece swing band.

Amongst the many other local groups are the long established Photographic Society, a Civic Society, a Local History Research Group and a Rotary Club. The local carnival, dating back to 1921 when it was organised by the Market Gardeners Association, is held in July and attracts many thousands; equally, the recently established Melbourne Arts and Music Festival is held in September and also brings several thousand people to the area.

The travel pioneer Thomas Cook was born in Melbourne in 1808; he started his business in Leicester in 1841 selling train excursions and taking a percentage of the railway tickets sold.

Melbourne has its own newspaper, the Village Voice, which has been in existence since 1992 under the guiding hand of David Bellis. It has expanded to include many neighbouring villages but Melbourne firmly remains at the centre of its publishing world.

Melbourne used to have its own brewery and, for a small population, a large and varied list of pubs. Even younger people can recall pubs no longer in existence and, talking to the older Melbourne residents, the names of the White Horse, Castle Inn, King's Head, Crewe and Harpur and the Sir Francis Burdett are likely to come into the conversation. Many landlords are fondly remembered for their liberal interpretation of their opening times; cricketers haven't always been able to buy a pint when the match finished early and had to play a 'beer' match until opening time was imminent. In its time the cricket club has used many, if not all, of the local pubs as a club base but, up until the 1970s, the Melbourne Hotel was the centre of its operations and its unofficial club house. With the sad decline of the brewing industry generally, even more Melbourne pubs are likely to close in the next 18 months. From fifteen pubs and clubs in the mid 1970s, the next few years may see that number drop to nine and of those only three will not be supported by a catering operation of some kind.

Melbourne people take a quiet pride in their town and think themselves fortunate to be living here and different from other Derbyshire people - not superior but just thankful that their lives led them to being here.

One Melbourne resident summed it up perfectly:
"If God made a better place, he kept it to himself."

THE APPEAL OF VILLAGE CRICKET AND LOCAL RIVALRY

"That doesn't make our local rivals disliked; far from it!"

It can be difficult explaining the appeal of village cricket to non-believers, especially in the current days of league-arranged fixtures where essentially you play where you are told.

In the past, when clubs were at the mercy of their Fixture Secretary, matches were arranged around favourite opponents, ease of travel, quality of grounds and last, but definitely not least, pubs. When asked by the Captain, prior to leaving for an away fixture, what the opposition were like, one Melbourne Fixture Secretary replied in all seriousness that their local did a decent drop of Ruddles County, were in the CAMRA beer guide and there was always the chance of a late drink.

There might be the indignity of changing in a converted farm building or railway carriage (Swarkestone have only just replaced theirs) and the possibility of standing on something that an animal has left behind in the outfield. The opposition might even harbour some long-standing grudge about which no-one can precisely remember the origins.

There's also the local rivalry that exists in other sports but in cricket it tends to be a lot more tense. All countries, counties and clubs have opponents that they compete against either regularly or sporadically. The hostility is played against a backdrop of a long-standing rivalry through either political history or geography. England has Australia, Pakistan has India, and Yorkshire has Lancashire. Every Robin Hood has a Sheriff of Nottingham, every Batman has a Joker and every Melbourne has a Ticknall (originally called Tichenhalle Cricket Club when they were formed, taking their name from the Anglo-Saxon name for the village). That doesn't make our local rivals disliked; far from it! There is a healthy respect for what they have achieved and the standard of cricket they currently play. In the past seasons our local rivals have played at the highest level in the Derbyshire League and our clubs' first elevens haven't competed against each other in quite a few seasons. However, there is no denying that when a Melbourne XI plays a Ticknall XI there is always an extra edge to the competition. Whether it is a Sunday friendly, the 3^{rd}XI or the 4^{th}XI it doesn't make the match any the less passionate; probably more so as the chance for one-upmanship and local bragging rights doesn't come along that often. Surprisingly, as our near neighbours are only a 20 minute walk away, we didn't play against each other until the 1951 season when Melbourne re-formed after a break for World War 2. A simple explanation is that prewar, Ticknall played in the Burton leagues and Melbourne in the Derby equivalent.

Breedon CC 1956 - at the time the premier local cricket team
Rear L-R: Bill Grewcock, John Danvers, David Jordan,
Mick Davis, Ralph Hallam, Bas Farmer, Maurice Harvey, Walter Watts.
Front L-R, Kevin Wilmore, Mick Wakefield, John Shields, Arnold Townsend,
Ken Danvers. (5)

Our other local rivals, Breedon on the Hill, are sadly no longer in existence. Based around the Breedon and Cloud Hill works, the club was originally organised by Captain C F Shields, who was managing director of the company and then later by his son, John. In the 1950s they regularly drew crowds of 2,000 spectators to their small ground at the Berryfield. They attracted many county players to their ranks (no professional Sunday cricket existed at the time), including Arnold Townsend, Norman West, Alan Revill and George Dawkes from Derbyshire and Don Munden from Leicestershire. Another Derby player was Albert Mays who also captained Derby County at football. Although Breedon had the playing stature of a minor counties side, they sadly disbanded in 1968 but not before the current Melbourne Vice Chairman and now 2nd XI bowler, Colin Wakefield, played for them. The Wakefield family were heavily involved in the club and many of Colin's relations captained the side including his uncle Lol and father Mick. Surprisingly, as with Ticknall, Melbourne didn't play against Breedon until 1954.

In the past, at the County and the Racecourse grounds in Derby, there were pitches whose outer boundaries crossed each other with the result that fielding 3rd man on one pitch would put you at deep mid-off on the next pitch. That left you with the uneasy feeling of trying to concentrate on the match you were playing whilst keeping one eye over your shoulder, watching the other game in case of a ball being smashed your way.

Then there's that sense of foreboding that hangs over every average player: this could be the afternoon when you are out for a duck, don't get a chance to bowl and drop an important catch. Adding to the day's feeling of rough justice, you will still be expected to part with your match subscriptions. It will be the same monetary amount as your team colleague's who has taken five wickets, two catches and scored 100 runs – proof positive that all things are equal in finance, but not in cricket.

On top of all this, you could stand as a strictly neutral umpire and have to rule on a tricky LBW, find in favour of your side's batsman and suffer the expletive deleted mutterings of the fielding side. How many of us have stood on the boundary, wishing that the opposition would put us out of our misery so we could get to the pub for the extracurricular part of cricket that players of all standards can enjoy?

You can wallow in the misery of all of the above, but the summer game can just as easily inspire. Sometimes it can be a great comfort to find that, thankfully, you are not surrounded by super-fit athletes.

Melbourne cricketers have seen six hits go on to car roofs, break pavilion tiles and windows, disappear into the allotments, into the score box and once onto a trailer disappearing out of Hattons's Yard and into the distance, heading for a local farm. That must have been the record for the biggest hit ever seen! With a bit of luck, allied to a modicum of skill (but not much), you might get some runs, not all as snicks through the slips, but the result of a textbook cover drive or meaty pull through midwicket.

There is something rather rewarding about being out in the sunshine on a picturesque ground playing a very English game with like-minded colleagues and the even greater pleasure of sharing a post match pint with your team, your opponents and especially the umpire who gave you out.

No less a person than D W Jardine, Captain of the MCC during the now famous bodyline tour to Australia in 1932/33 and probably the greatest of all English Captains had this to say:

"It is the humbler manifestation which is infinitely more important for the sport as a whole and the choice between clicking turnstiles and the village green is, in reality, no choice at all: the village has it every time."

DEFINITIONS OF CRICKET

"The dismissal of a batsman is a bowler's attempt
at a dot ball which didn't go quite to plan"

It's one thing to play the game and another to play it well, but how many of us have often struggled to explain what happens in a cricket match - especially to an American? At the lunch interval during a match at Lord's in the 1950s, spectator Groucho Marx was asked what he thought of the game.

"Great!" he replied, "When does it start?" If you have either a few minutes to spare, the whole afternoon or a minimum of one pint after the match, the following two explanations may help with your conversational partner's enlightenment. The second is only to be used if you have a night to spare as the answer will be followed by many more questions. Use the first one if in a hurry.

1.   The man with the bat tries to hit the ball to a fielder; if he doesn't succeed then he must run up and down the wicket as punishment.
2.   You have two sides, one out in the field and one in. Each man that's in the side that's in goes out, and when he's out he comes in and the next man goes in until he's out. When they are all out, the side that's out comes in and the side that's been in goes out and tries to get those coming in, out. Sometimes you get men still in and not out. When a man goes out to go in, the men who are out try to get him out, and when he is out he goes in and the next man in goes out and goes in. There are two men called umpires who stay out all the time and they decide when the men who are in are out. When both sides have been in and all the men have been out, and both sides have been out twice after all the men have been in, including those who are not out, that is the end of the game.

Then there are the endlessly complicated definitions of what happens in the game. Apollo 14 astronaut Marvin Mitchell claimed there is life out there and aliens have already made contact with us. Here are fourteen extraterrestrial explanations that can be used when the flying saucer lands at the cricket ground. Where there is a Melbourne context there is a further, shortened explanation at the end. Specific names can be found in the player profile section in Chapter 18.

1.   An appeal is a 250 decibel scream made to overcome the obvious hereditary and professional deafness so common in the umpiring profession. See Steve Price.

Victorious captain
Steve (Asda) Price with the Lothian trophy,
presented by club patron Lord Ralph Kerr. (6)

2. "Givitsumwelly!" is a mysterious, almost religious chant that comes out of the mouth of the cricket spectator. Sometimes it can be repeated by one person 1200 times in an afternoon, especially if the opposing players are batting. It can usually be heard on away grounds, more often than not in the areas of Burton and North Derbyshire.

3. Football is a crude winter game played with inflated pigskin. It provides much tedious talk in the cricket dressing room when raining, in newspapers, at the Alma Inn and on Radio Derby. If particular care is not taken, the chatter will worsen and the desire will arise to play the 'beautiful' game all year round.

4. Bits and pieces player: a cricketer who is only average at more things than the average player.

5. The dismissal of a batsman is a bowler's attempt at a dot ball which didn't go quite to plan.

6. A fielding circle is a lot of dots which, if joined up, would not make a circle.

7. Fielding restrictions are ways of making Captains put fielders where they don't want them.

8. The one-day shot is a heave across line unlikely to make contact with ball, thereby scoring no runs and making batsman liable to be bowled; it is played by a batsman in the belief that this helps him to score runs quickly.

9. Running the ball down to third man is a way to make batting harder by using less of the bat's face. This shot is now unused in Melbourne cricket; people trying this in the past have always been caught behind by the wicketkeeper or failed to make contact.

10. The required run-rate is something batsmen early in an innings increase, leaving their bowlers later in the innings to decrease.

11. A spinner is a medium pacer with a shorter than usual run-up.

12. A stonewaller is a very senior player trying to recapture nonexistent past glories. See Andy Heafield.

13. A slip is what happens to a fielder without spikes on wet grass.

14. A wicketkeeper is a batsman who keeps his pads on when fielding. See Ken Grant.

TEL'S LAW
MELBOURNE CRICKET'S 10 COMMANDMENTS

"Drunk or hungover might just be tolerated as an excuse for lateness"

Cut through club Chairman and former player, Tel Potts and you will find, as in the finest stick of rock, 'Melbourne' stamped through the middle. Keeper of the club principles and with wife Sue's assistance, he is the cornerstone of the club's foundations. The 10 Commandments have been written with him in mind; there was no visit to the mountain to find these, just many hours in his company over pints of Marston's Pedigree at the Melbourne Royal British Legion.

Three generations in one match
Chairman Tel Potts (right) with son Dave and grandson Harry at the Melbourne legends of cricket, 2010. (7)

1. Always go to winter nets; that way you won't be accused of being a player who simply turns up at the start of the season and expects to bat, bowl and field at slip.
2. Offer to help with the pitch; there's always something to do. Don't expect to be given the mower; there's an established order to these things and to be given the mower is something to aspire to in the future.
3. Don't throw a wobbler if you have to bat number nine or bowl third change. It could be worse: bat number eleven; field at third man both ends and don't bowl.
4. Always offer to do the tea even if it's on behalf of your wife, better half or partner. It's the best way to impress team-mates and far easier than taking all 10 wickets or making a quick 50. Does it matter if you are selected for your teas rather than your cricketing ability? The added bonus is that your wife's tea-making ability is likely to last longer than your cricketing career.
5. Always offer to umpire, if you are able, but don't be tempted to win popularity by being biased. It'll backfire as soon as you come into bat. And you get the chance to wear a white coat and lose count every over.
6. Don't drop out on the evening before a match or even one hour prior to the start. All excuses have been heard before: car broken down, called into work, children kidnapped, wife divorcing you, terrorists holding you hostage - are no justification for letting your cricket colleagues down. Drunk or hungover might just be tolerated as an excuse for lateness!
7. Pay your match fees on the day. Your Captain cannot be expected to run a 12 entry ledger system and anyway, he'll probably be going for a drink afterwards and is bound to forget who has paid, or more importantly who has not.
8. Don't talk yourself up or you're sure to be a disappointment not only to yourself but to your colleagues. In football, how many people, especially Geordies, have you heard say that they have had a trial for Newcastle only to fall over from a total lack of skill and an over indulgence of Mars Bars and Newcastle Brown Ale? It's the same in cricket; just do the opposite and tell the skipper that you bat middle to late order, have been known to bowl and are a keen fielder. That way, your new colleagues will be pleasantly surprised when you knock off a ton, take 5 wickets and

generally field like a gazelle. On the downside, you will be expected to buy jugs of beer for your newly impressed cricketing friends. The beer will impress them as much as, if not more than, your cricketing skills.

9. Clap and cajole lots in the field, even if some of the performances are somewhat below standard. You'll want encouragement when you are performing so do no less when someone else is.

10. Never, ever, take yourself too seriously. There's a queue of people waiting to bring you down to earth with a well aimed comment that will usually take place at the time of maximum embarrassment.

Rather like that other bringer of Commandments, Tel looks after his flock and we all hope that, after many years spent in the sporting wilderness, he will be leading us to the Promised Land via promotion up the cricketing ladder. The analogy doesn't end there either: never, ever, forget the 11th unwritten and most important commandment,

"Thou shalt always beat Ticknall!"

CLUB HISTORY

"Kettledrum won the Epsom Derby"

If you add up all the numbers between two and seven, the total is twenty seven, the coloured balls in snooker have a total value of twenty seven and there are twenty seven books in the New Testament of the Bible. Here are twenty seven facts about the year 1861.

1. It was the start of the American Civil War that lasted until 1865.
2. Abraham Lincoln made his inaugural speech.
3. An earthquake completely destroyed Mendoza in Argentina.
4. China was in the midst of a civil war.
5. William Wrigley, the chewing gum industrialist was born.
6. The English poet, Elizabeth Barratt Browning, died.
7. Queen Victoria celebrated her 42nd birthday.
8. Storms damaged the Crystal Palace in London.
9. Crystal Palace Football Club was formed.
10. It was the start of the Lancashire cotton famine.
11. Mrs Beeton published her book of Household Management.
12. The 1st Earl Haig was born.
13. Prince Albert, husband of Queen Victoria, died.
14. Tom Morris senior won the Open Golf Championship.
15. Jealousy won the Grand National.
16. Oxford won the 18th University Boat Race.
17. Kettledrum won the Epsom Derby.
18. 'Abide with me' was written and published.
19. Jem Mace won the heavyweight boxing championship of England.
20. Famous opera singer, Dame Nellie Melba, was born.
21. James Naismith invented the sport of basketball.
22. W G Grace celebrated his 13th birthday and was one year away from making his county debut.

23. An English cricket touring team travelled to Australia for the first time, captained by H H Stephenson.
24. Derby County Football Club was still twenty three years away from being founded in 1884.
25. Derbyshire County Cricket Club was nine years away from being founded in 1870.
26. Melbourne born Thomas Cook ran the first package holiday from London to Paris.
27. Melbourne Town Cricket Club played its first game.

Beginnings

"It wasn't until 1864 that over arm bowling
as we know it today was legalised"

The exact origins of cricket are unknown, but it certainly dates back to the 16th century. The name is thought to have originated from the Anglo-Saxon word cricc, meaning a shepherd's staff. The first players were thought to be the shepherds of south-east England, who used their crooks as bats and the wicket gate and movable bail of the sheep pens as a target for the bowlers.

Early cricketers played in their everyday clothes and had no protective equipment such as gloves or pads. A 1743 painting of a game in progress depicts two batsmen and a bowler dressed alike in white shirt, breeches, white knee-length stockings and shoes with buckles. The wicketkeeper wears the same clothes, with the addition of a waistcoat. An umpire and scorer wear three-quarter length coats and tricorn hats. Apart from the shirts and stockings, none of the clothes are white and no one wears pads or gloves. The ball is bowled along the ground, as in bowls, at varying speed towards a wicket consisting of two stumps mounted by a single crosspiece. The batsman addresses the delivery with a bat that resembles a modern hockey stick, this shape being ideal for dealing with a ball on the ground.

Mention of the following words and phrases in 1861 would have been met with a blank look: sledging, limited overs match, 20/20, bodyline, the googly, the Ashes, sight screen, a flipper, helmet, test match, pinch hitter and finally, one for Melbourne cricketers of every generation, Ticknall Cricket Club, as they weren't formed until the late 1800s. Melbourne Town Cricket Club was therefore one nil up early on in battles with our long standing local rivals. In some cricket reports of the Derby Mercury in the 1860s, the sport is referred to as caicket.

Cricket in those days wasn't so far removed from the cricket of today if you strip away the helmets, thigh pads, bats the size of railway sleepers and 20/20. Batsmen batted and bowlers bowled although round arm bowling was still the action of the day. It wasn't until 1864 that over arm bowling as we know it today was legalised. It was still 11 men against 11. In local cricket it wasn't uncommon for villages to have several cricket teams; sides representing employers, churches, chapels, local areas and even families would regularly compete against each other for local bragging rights. This led to sides being chosen to represent their village when playing against neighbouring villages. Ultimately, these sides became the focal points of village sporting life and the teams that the better players would naturally want to play for.

It was a golden age of cricket in those Victorian times and society embraced the sport which rapidly became our national game. The game itself developed even further and in many minds combined the British traits of manliness, good temperament, a healthy mind and body and overriding all of that, fair play. On the pitch, developments included the use of the heavy roller to improve pitches, the introduction of boundaries, the standardisation of the rules by the MCC, the expansion of cricket grounds to accommodate an increasing number of spectators and the hitherto unheard of, team dress. Something that still strikes a chord today was that the Victorians' love affair with cricket had much to do with the ever-advancing industrial changes taking place; not everyone welcomed technological change and cricket offered a way of keeping in touch with the village green and a more romanticised view of England.

Early Days

"Who would have thought that cricketing ringers
would exist in 1871?"

Some of the early matches in which the club participated are recorded in the Derby Mercury, the foremost County newspaper of the day. The reports do not cover each match or year and appear sporadically but it can be confirmed that the club played matches against Long Whatton in 1863, Alvaston in 1869, Ashby in 1870 (the Ashby team being Captained by the Marquis of Hastings), Worthington in 1870 and Kegworth in 1871. At some point there must have been some internal strife at the club as one match report from August 24th 1870 reports that a game took place at the Mount Pleasant ground between two teams, one representing the club and another representing Saint Michael's Church. In reading between the lines, it appears that early in the season some members of the club did not entirely agree with how the organisation was run and formed themselves into a separate team based at Saint Michael's Church. The report goes on to appeal for the two clubs to once more combine their forces:

"Unfortunately the members of the club are mainly, if not entirely, composed of working men to whom the expenses attending the matches are often a serious item ...... the encouragement given to the club by two of England's greatest statesmen and the interest taken in this noble and truly national game by every class of society bringing them into association or contact from the cobblers stall to the palace, the peasant and the peer leads me to hope that our worthy vicar, Lord Cooper, Mrs Gooch and Mrs Fox will use their influence to promote a union of the two clubs."

The two statesmen are not identified by name and neither is the writer of the report. The reunion strategy obviously failed as some ten years later, in their issue of March 24th 1880, the same newspaper refers to the Annual General meeting of St Michaels Cricket and Quoits Club. The last paragraph states very grandly that the noblest of English games will not be wanting in zeal and support.

In many of the reports it is noted that a spacious marquee was erected by Mr Warren of the New Inn (now the Melbourne Hotel) and an excellent luncheon was served. A match report from the July 29th 1874 edition of the Mercury, when Melbourne entertained a team from H Allsopp's company in Derby, comments that H Allsopp not only organised his team but drove the members with a brake and four bays.

Another Mercury report of August 1875 states that Melbourne employed a professional cricketer, a C Randon, who in the match against a Derby XI bowled 9 over's for nine runs and took 6 wickets. Melbourne batted first and were bowled out for 41, their opponents for a mere 21. This is the only recorded instant of a paid professional cricketer representing the club.

In a sign that very little ever happens in modern cricket that hasn't been replicated many times over, on October 4th in 1871 a certain Mr Perambulator appeared for the club playing against Mr Wilisford's Estate XI. He scored 47 runs out of a total of 92 as Melbourne won by 36 runs. With his surname and apparent ability, there is every chance that Mr Perambulator may have been appearing under an assumed name. Who would have thought that cricketing ringers would have existed in 1871?

Fundraising was then, as it still is, a major part of the club's activities. There was the usual staple diet of dances and dinners but very unusually the Derby Mercury Christmas issue of 1887 reports that the Midlands Dramatic Company were paying a return visit to the town where the performances would include "Leah the Jewish Maiden" and "The Bookworm". The performance took place at the Athanaeum room in Potter Street with half the receipts of the Thursday and Friday performances being given to the cricket club. The dramatic and musical theme carried on as, in March 1889, a concert was given in MTCC funds: amongst the poems, recitals and musical performances was a song by Mr John Horsley titled Monarch of the Woods. John Horsley was the father of Jim Horsley (see Ch. 10 - MTCC Legend and County Cricketer). Another fund raiser was an open athletics meeting jointly organised by the cricket club and the Melbourne Cycling Club in 1891. The Mercury reports that the organisers were disappointed with the attendance of "only" 600 spectators. The event was held in a meadow owned by Mr Knowles near the Hall gardens and a special train was run from Derby to carry competitors and their supporters.

The Andrews family played a large part in the early 1900s and the Derby Mercury reports that J F and A E Andrews opened the batting and bowling on many occasions. Against Derby Midland in July 1910 they took 9 wickets between them, J F scoring 52 runs. They also played for Melbourne in the Derby and District League and when the club were champions in 1907, 1908 and 1912.

In 1910, Jim Horsley, later to play for Nottinghamshire and Derbyshire, is recorded on the scorecard of Albert E Andrews as taking four catches. Also recorded on that scorecard, with their number of catches in brackets, are: Albert E Andrews (2), Arthur (7), Jack (7), E Tivey (1), Rowlate (9), Wilson (4), L Coxon (2) and M Coxon (4).

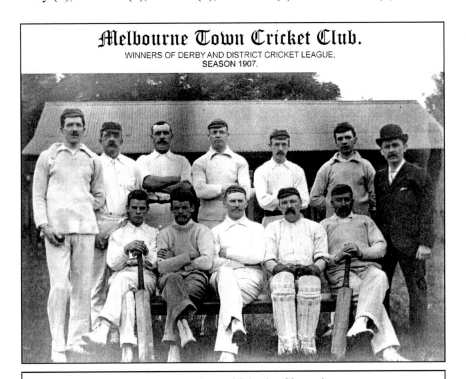

Melbourne Town Cricket Club.
WINNERS OF DERBY AND DISTRICT CRICKET LEAGUE; SEASON 1907.

The 1907 Derby and District Champions
Rear L-R: A E Andrews, J W Blood, J H Knipe, E Tivey,
J F Andrews, Albert E Andrews, A J Hatton.
Front L-R: R C Tivey, S E Tivey, E Salsbury, F J Illsley, F Wilson. (8)

The season of 1912 had to be decided by a play off between Spondon CC and the MTCC, an epic match which had to be played over two days with a week between each day and at two different venues.

On the first Saturday of the match, played at the County Ground in Derby, the MTCC batted and were all out for 157, a total that was reached with the immense contribution of J F Andrews who made 107 runs. At the close of play, Spondon had made 40 for 2. On the following Saturday, the match continued at the Railway Ground in Derby and Spondon were bowled out for the addition of another 32 runs. An inscribed silver cigarette case was later presented to 'J F' in recognition of his fine innings. He was a member of the Andrews family that contributed to cricket in Melbourne from the late 1800s to the 1970s. Records show that players from the 1907 Championship side were: E Salisbury (Captain), A E Andrews, J W Blood, J H Knipe, E Tivey, J F Andrews, E Andrews, F C Tivey, S E Tivey, E J Illsley and J Wilson: the scorer was A J Hatton.

Cricket was also seen during these times as social glue. Whilst the country was beset by national unrest, organised labour and politics, cricket had an unmatched mixture of all social classes: Lords playing alongside butlers, bank managers alongside their clerks and land owners with their labourers. Anything that put such economically different people on common ground and playing together for the collective good was seen as beneficial.

The MTCC team flourished between the wars and in 1928, J F Andrews was rewarded by the club for 30 years' continuous service as Club Secretary with a piece of Royal Crown Derby. A descendant of the family, Hugh Andrews, was the club Vice Chairman in the 1960s. Players from those prewar days included the proprietor of the Gayborder Nurseries, the sons of the local vicar and headmasters of both the National schools, in the High Street and in Penn Lane. In 1939, the club disbanded for the duration of World War 2. At one point the ground was destined to be ploughed up and used for the war effort but many of the cricket club members who were still in Melbourne rallied against this and it didn't happen.

Starting Again

"His party piece to the assembled crowd was taking
the tops off bottles of beer with his teeth"

After World War 2, the club was re-started in 1950. Doctor Hedley
Boardman and Gerry Shaw, both lifelong cricket lovers, called a public
meeting with only one item on the agenda:
"The Reformation of Melbourne Town Cricket Club".

Cricket Is Back
After a 12 year break, the official re-opening of the ground on
May 12th 1951 is performed by Mr Clarence Bell accompanied
by Mr Ronnie Loake and Dr Hedley Boardman. (9)

Many of the prewar players supported the cause, fund raising events
were arranged and the considerable task of getting the long neglected
ground, wicket and pavilion in good condition was started. Working

parties were organised and expert advice from Derbyshire Cricket Club was sought to ensure correct treatment of the wicket. The autumn, winter and early spring of the years 1950/51 saw great activity at the cricket ground – mowing, hand rolling, top dressing of the wicket, painting, joinery and bricklaying were all carried out by club members and volunteers. A water pipe was laid from Hatton's Yard in Hope Street to the pavilion, the trench being dug out entirely by hand; no JCB machinery was available then!

As a result of the great enthusiasm and hard work, the ground was ready for the opening match against J Parker and Sons from Derby on May 12th 1951. The opening ball of the match was ceremonially bowled by the local Justice of The Peace, Clarence Bell. The Melbourne team players are featured in the photo below.

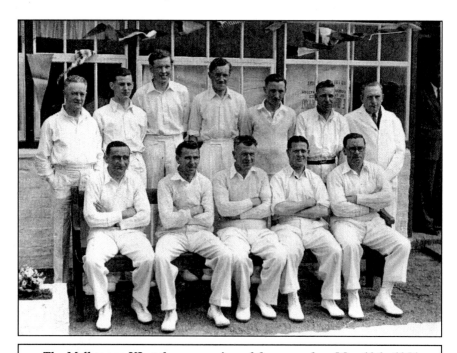

The Melbourne XI at the re-opening of the ground on May 12th, 1951
The team that day was R J Blood, G Brunton, J K Draper, E Dunnicliff,
F Dunnicliff (captain), S Gray, J R Hatton, R K Hatton, J K Keith-Reid,
R J Robinson, , G Shaw, and G Ensor (umpire). (10)

Team selection in the 1950s and 1960s was radically different to the email, Twitter, Facebook, mobile phone and texting processes that now dominate team selection. Players were very parochial and members usually lived and worked in and around the area. A playing list was on display in the pavilion and you simply ticked your availability. Captains would meet at the Melbourne Hotel on a Tuesday evening and teams would be picked from the list. By Wednesday lunchtime the teams were on display on the notice board in the Market Place. If you had a car, you were usually one of the first on the team sheet as transport and getting to the match was sometimes put before cricketing promise. Occasionally, the team travelled by public transport, a Trent bus to Derby and then a change for another bus to the venue. A simple operation you would think but for one 'small' detail! Back then there was no individual kit, just a team kit bag which contained at least five pairs of pads, assorted batting gloves, umpires' coats, bats, balls and wicketkeeper's kit. It took two burly cricketers to carry it anywhere, and this had to be taken to each match.

The First Ball
*Ceremonially bowled by Clarence Bell with umpire George Ensor
on hand to ensure a legal delivery. (11)*

CRICKET TEAM SHEET

THE FOLLOWING PLAYERS HAVE BEEN SELECTED TO PLAY AGAINST

COALVILLE

at _MELBOURNE_

on _SATURDAY   SEPTEMBER 9_ TH

> J TURNER (Captain)
> R GRUMMETT
> D HOARE
> D DUNNICLIFFE
> T POTTS
> D CALVERT
> C TOON
> J HALLIFIELD
> M HARVEY
> P WAKEFIELD
> L BARBER

RESERVES _UMPIRE   F ASHMORE_
SCORER   M BAREHAM

RENDEZVOUS _GROUND_
TIME _2.00 PM._
TRANSPORT ARRANGEMENTS ARE _____

HARRY   SAMMY
ELLIOTT & CROOKS
SPORTS OUTFITTERS
Tel. 43169   44, OSMASTON ROAD (The Spot), DERBY   Tel. 43169

Left: No electronic mail in those days. Team sheets were pinned up every week in the Market Place.(12)

Below. If you couldn't get to read the team sheet, you received a postcard. (13)

MELBOURNE TOWN CRICKET CLUB.

Match Secretary :
J. K. DRAPER,

3, Station Road,
Melbourne, Derby.
Tel. Derby 46003 (Business)

Dear Sir,

You have been selected to play for the _1st_ eleven

on _Saturday 21/7/51 @ 3pm_ against _Swarkestone_

at _Swarkestone_   Transport _TRENT SERVICE BUS_

If you cannot play, please let me know before Friday.

Yours faithfully,

J. K. DRAPER.

In the 1950s the club hosted Derbyshire benefit matches for two county stalwarts, A E G (Dusty) Rhodes and Cliff Gladwin. Dusty played for the county from 1937 and 1954 and went on to umpire internationally. Cliff Gladwin played for the county between 1939 and 1958 and represented his country eight times. The benefit teams for both matches included Derek Morgan, a cricketing all-rounder who went on to captain Derbyshire and reach the double of 10,000 runs and 1,000 wickets for the county and Joe Hardstaff junior from Nottinghamshire, who had played 23 times for England. Donald Carr also played in both matches; he was the Derbyshire Captain between 1955 and 1962 and an England player. He captained the MCC in India and went on to be assistant Secretary of the same organisation. Carr also played in the FA Amateur Cup Final twice for Pegasus, who won on both occasions. George Dawkes, the Leicestershire and Derbyshire wicketkeeper, who also toured India as a part of a Commonwealth XI, was behind the stumps.

Heads Or Tails
The two captains in the A E Rhodes testimonial match.
(14)

Committee minutes of the time show that there was considerable debate over the selection of the Melbourne team. For the match against the Dusty Rhodes XI, it was decided that, given the quality of the opposition, players from other clubs would be invited to appear for a Melbourne and

District team in an effort (quoting from the minutes) "to give a good account of ourselves". Therefore, the Melbourne team included B Hall (Wirksworth), N West (Draycott), G Edwards and H Wheatley (both of Derby), F J Brooks and K Roberts (both of Burton). A similar debate was held before the Cliff Gladwin XI match that reached the same conclusion. The Melbourne team for that match included M F Pickett, C Tate, J Hancock, D Green (all from Burton), R Huggins (from the RAF) and a 17 year old Harold Rhodes, who went on to play for Derbyshire and England. Melbourne umpire for both games was George Ensor; the other umpire was another Derbyshire cricket legend, Les Jackson, who only played two tests for England, despite being widely acknowledged as the finest fast-bowler of his generation. His two test appearances were 12 years apart in 1949 and 1961; he was undoubtedly the victim of prejudice against certain counties that existed in those days. Les is also remembered when, at the dance held at the Public Hall following the Rhodes testimonial, he demonstrated his party piece to the assembled crowd, taking the tops off bottles of beer with his teeth. That would have impressed the grandees at Lords!

Just For Openers
The opening batsmen for the A E Rhodes XI. (15)

Following the Rhodes benefit, a cricket bat was given to the club, to be awarded to the most improved young player at the club. According to the club's minutes, "after much discussion," it was awarded to Roy Grummett. Roy would have been about 17 years old at the time and went on to play for the club into the 1990s. Whether he was still using the same bat is a matter of debate. Minutes from a committee meeting held in 1952 show that the testimonial for Dusty Rhodes raised the princely sum of 74 pounds 10 shillings and five pence. How times have changed: the average wage for an agricultural labourer was six pounds a week. That sum raised in 1952 is the equivalent of just over £ 6,000 now. A picture (page 43) from the match shows the entire boundary being ringed by spectators and their cars and a flagpole with the union flag flying proudly next to the pavilion. Sadly, the flagpole has not been a feature at the ground for many years but plans are afoot to bring it back in all its glory.

England, Derbyshire and Melbourne
Umpires Les Jackson,
(Derbyshire and England)
left and George Ensor,
(Melbourne) right, walk
out prior to the
testimonial match for
A E (Dusty) Rhodes. Les
was later to star at the
post match reception. (16)

A E Rhodes Testimonial - The Melbourne and District XI
George Ensor (Umpire, rear left) and players F J Brooks, A Dickman,
G Edwards, R Gray, B Hall, J Houghton, V Jackson, K Roberts, C Toon,
N West, H Wheatley. (17)

The A E Rhodes XI team
Players: T R Armstrong, D B Carr, G Dawkes, C S Eliott, A Hamer,
J Hardstaff, J Kelly, D C Morgan, A C Revill, A E Rhodes, G L Willatt. (18)

Melbourne and District XI

R. GRAY,   Melbourne

B. HALL,   Wirksworth

F. J. BROOKS,   Burton

K. ROBERTS,   Burton

N. WEST,   Draycott

G. EDWARDS,   Derby

V. JACKSON,   Melbourne

J. HOUGHTON,   Melbourne

C. TOON,   Melbourne

H. WHEATLEY,   Derby

A. DICKMAN,   Melbourne

Umpires :

G. Ensor   L. Jackson
(Melbourne)   (Derbyshire)

A. E. RHODES'
TESTIMONIAL

MELBOURNE
JULY 6TH, 1952

SOUVENIR CARD

A. E. RHODES' XI   AUTOGRAPHS

C. S. ELLIOTT

A. HAMER

A. E. RHODES

J. HARDSTAFF (Notts.)

A. C. REVILL

D. B. CARR

J. KELLY

G. L. WILLATT

D. C. MORGAN

G. DAWKES

T. R. ARMSTRONG

Autographed card from the A E Rhodes match (19)

Melbourne and District XI

M. F. PICKETT   Burton C.C.
C. TATE   ,,
J. HANCOCK   ,,
D. GREEN   ,,
H. RHODES   Derbyshire C.C.C.
G. EDWARDS   County Offices
R. HUGGINS   ex R.A.F.
M. A. NEWBERY Melbourne C.C.
C. CLAYTON   ,,
D. DUNNICLIFFE   ,,
J. HOUGHTON   ,,

Umpire: G. Ensor   Scorer: H. Draper

E. H. Beardsley, Printer, Commerce St., Melbourne

Cliff Gladwin

Testimonial Cricket Match

MELBOURNE TOWN CRICKET GROUND
SUNDAY, 5th JULY, 1953

Souvenir Card

CLIFF GLADWINS XI

G. L. WILLATT
D. B. CARR
C. S. ELLIOTT
A. HAMER
J. KELLY
A. E. G. RHODES
A. C. REVILL
G. O. DAWKES
C. GLADWIN
D. C. MORGAN
L. JACKSON

E. SMITH 12th man

AUTOGRAPHS

Autographed card from the Cliff Gladwin match (20)

Never Fuller
The ground at the A E Rhodes testimonial. Cars were circling the
ground. The crowd was estimated at over one thousand. (21)

We all tend to take cricket teas for granted, yet in the fifties, teas had to be organised to strict restrictions as post war rationing was still in operation. The club had to make an annual declaration to the Ministry of Food; failure to do so would have resulted in a court appearance for the club Secretary and a possible jail sentence! Very few Sunday matches were held during this time mainly due to the food rationing but also because permission was required from the parish council to hold sporting contests on the Sabbath.

The Annual General Meeting held in 1951 discussed problems with cricketers retrieving cricket balls from the adjoining allotments, player selection, the repair of the sightscreens and the football season encroaching into the cricket season: some 60 years later these 'hot' topics are still on the agenda. The annual subscription of 10 shillings (50p) a year was felt to be a high price and members were allowed to pay in monthly instalments.

It is widely thought by many good judges of local cricket that the club's golden era was between 1958 and 1966 under the Captaincy of Fred Bentley. During this period, the club reached the final of the Butterley Cup in 1965, which was played against Aitons Welfare at the old International Combustion ground in Sinfin Lane, Derby. The MTCC lost that final in a hard fought match, Aitons scoring 97 runs and Melbourne

Melbourne 1st XI 1963
*Rear L-R: Fred Bentley, Harold Draper, Lennie Barber, Frank Ashmore,
Roy Grummett, Clive Burton, Malcom Spare, Richard Hatton, John Turner,
Dennis Dunnicliffe, Charles (Bud) Toon, Mick Clough, Harold Hodgkinson.
Front L-R: Tel Potts, Graham Whyatt, Mrs Kirkman, Sylvia Griffiths,
Barbara Hatton, Mrs Turner, Brenda Bentley, Mrs Dunnicliffe.
Sitting on the ground: Lynn Bentley, Christina Dunnicliffe. (22)*

failing narrowly to reach that target, only scoring 92 runs despite some
mighty blows from Bas Farmer. The club reached the semi final the
following year, played at Swarkestone. but once again we were defeated.
How was the club to know that we wouldn't reach another cup final until
2010? After that semi final defeat, Fred Bentley stood down as Captain
after eight years to be replaced by his Vice Captain John Turner who went
on to Captain the 1st XI for many years. Many cricketers from that era also
recall John's mother, known to many as only 'Mrs Turner', who was the
club's tea lady. In the late 1950s and through to the mid 1960s, the Ronnie
Loake Cup was a very popular inter-company tournament, organised by
the club and open to organisations in the area. Melbourne Engineering, the
Liberal Club, Nixon and Knowles, Dunnicliff's and the British Legion all
entered teams.

        During this period, in 1960, a youngster started playing for the club;
as with many players new to the club he had to be patient and content
himself with the odd game during his first season, but it would be the start
of a long relationship with the MTCC for current Chairman, Tel Potts.

Melbourne Town 1st XI, 1962
Rear L-R: George Ensor, George Massey, Derek Tomlinson, Malcom Spare,
Charles (Bud) Toon, Roy Grummett, Pete Clough.
Front L-R: John Turner, Dennis Dunnicliffe, Fred Bentley,
Graham Whyatt, Lennie Barber. (23)

The Seventies and Beyond

"The long tradition of the beer match
Was destined to become history"

It was the era of flares, glam rock, the television detective series 'The Sweeney' and the horror film 'The Exorcist', yet if you look at team pictures from that era there seems very little to differentiate between players then and their illustrious predecessors. Players from the 1950s: Stan Hatton, Lennie Barber, Roy Grummett, and Richard Hatton, were still playing along with their younger counterparts from the swinging sixties, and new to the team youngsters such as Graham Leach and Stuart Pegg.

Melbourne 1st XI c 1975
*Rear L-R: Adrian Bradley (scorer), Graham Leech, Stan Hatton, Richard
Tivey, George Harris, Tom Jackson, Lennie Barber, Brian Spare (umpire).
Front L-R: Richard Hatton, John Dando, John Turner, David Baxter,
John Hallifield. (24)*

Then, as ever, Melbourne Cricket was a glorious mixture of
generations, ambitions, outlooks, careers and motivation. This cricketing
concoction was on splendid display at the annual dinners. The earliest
known annual dinner was in 1863 at the New Inn (now the Melbourne
Hotel), hosted by the innkeeper, Mr Upton, where, according to the Derby
Mercury, 36 people were present and enjoyed patriotic toasts with songs
from Messrs Upton, Tivey and Cook. The Hotel continued to be the club
room of the MTCC well into the 1970s under the patronage of the late
George Johnson. Since then they have been at almost every venue in the
area including the Public Hall, the Hall Tea Rooms and the Melbourne
View Hotel but have all followed the same successful format along the
lines of "if it ain't broke don't fix it!" Still remembered with much
amusement is when, in the mid seventies, in order to raise much needed
funds for the club, tickets were sold separately for the post dinner disco,
which was estimated to start at 9 pm. The dinner organisers hadn't

reckoned with then club Chairman Richard Hatton staying on his feet for a 40 minute Chairman's address, which went down well with the club membership, but not so well with the ever impatient queue of seventies clad disco dancers in the Autumn cold outside, who waited as Richard carried on, determined to finish the speech and reach his well prepared conclusion. The club dinner had many illustrious former Derbyshire players as guests including Derek Morgan, Peter Gibbs, Cliff Gladwin and Ian Anderson.

The year of 1978 was the first year since the re-formation of the club in 1951 that we had entered a league competition, the Derby and District Cricket League. Many members had fought against joining a league and had wanted to continue to play only in friendly matches, but due to the lack of potential opponents it was reluctantly accepted at the AGM of the previous year. A considerable number of members thought it was the end of the world! In that debut season, the 1st XI finished eighth out of eleven teams and the 2nd XI eighth out of nine. It was a tough league we had joined as witnessed by a 2nd XI match against Derby Congs in 1979. Our opponents reached a healthy 189 for seven wickets; Melbourne replied with six all out and that score included three extras. On the scoreboard that day with one run each were: W Swarbrook, K Sheldon and S Floyd. Those not troubling the scorers were: L Barber, G Twells, S Taylor, A Earp, R Lakin, K Woodward, J Blood and J Heath who was zero not out. The opponents' opening bowlers took five wickets for one run and five wickets for two runs respectively. However, in the same season, there were some good performances: in the league batting averages, Roy Grummett came fourth, averaging 33 with a top score of 70. In the bowling averages, Lennie Barber with 32 wickets and John Hallifield with 31 wickets came fourth and seventh respectively.

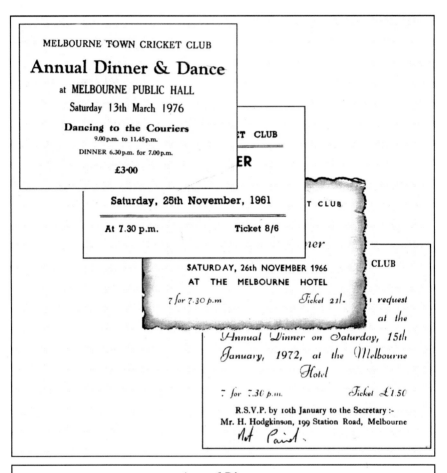

MELBOURNE TOWN CRICKET CLUB

Annual Dinner & Dance

at MELBOURNE PUBLIC HALL

Saturday 13th March 1976

Dancing to the Couriers
9.00 p.m. to 11.45 p.m.

DINNER 6.30 p.m. for 7.00 p.m.

£3·00

Saturday, 25th November, 1961

At 7.30 p.m.   Ticket 8/6

SATURDAY, 26th NOVEMBER 1966
AT   THE   MELBOURNE   HOTEL

7 for 7.30 p.m   Ticket 21/-

Annual Dinner on Saturday, 15th January, 1972, at the Melbourne Hotel

7 for 7.30 p.m.   Ticket £1.50

R.S.V.P. by 10th January to the Secretary :-
Mr. H. Hodgkinson, 199 Station Road, Melbourne

Not Paid.

Annual Dinners
A dinner for less than the current price of a half pint. (25)

A club dinner from the 1950s
Formal invitations meant formal dress. (26)

It was in the 1980s that another great change came about in village cricket: the extension of the licensing hours to enable pubs to open all day, enabling cricketers to buy a pint if their game finished in a batting collapse. It also meant that the long tradition of the beer match was destined to become history. Generations of cricketers would be denied the opportunity to have a 10 over thrash with the batting order being reversed: the beer match's sole purpose was to fill in the time between the primary match finishing and the bolts on the pub door being slid back. As with all things cricket, timing was everything. There was nothing distinguished about the beer match; it was good for a laugh, not to be taken too seriously, a good chance for a hit and hope swing of the willow and for the non bowlers to have a few overs. Just to show that nothing is ever new, a genius in the marketing department of cricket's governing body decided to slightly tinker with the rules of the beer match; play in bright clothes, stick a hot tub on the boundary, introduce rock music and call it 20/20. Amazingly, it caught on!

In the 1980s, the club also hosted the annual Melbourne pub cricket festival. Like the beer match, it was a simple format: six a side cricket in a knock out format with teams being drawn from the pubs of Melbourne. Pubs could only have a minimum of three cricketers on each team: it was a very popular format with cricketers and spectators alike.

The late 1990s and early 2000s saw many of the club stalwarts declare their long innings and go into semi-retirement. Tel Potts, Roy Grummett, Richard Hatton, George Harris, Lennie Barber and Stan Hatton had over 200 years of playing experience between them and they were not easily replaced. However, in the mid 2000s the club achieved successive promotions under the captaincy of Alex Slater; unfortunately the club was unable to build on that success and at one point towards the end of the decade nearly disbanded the second team. The MTCC undoubtedly paid the price for not having any junior sides whilst their near neighbours at Ticknall and Swarkestone reaped the benefits of having successful junior development policies. Without a doubt, those two clubs were also helped by being able to develop the facilities at their grounds. Melbourne cricket has been slow to realise that present day cricketers like new and up to date facilities: what was once seen as a luxury is now regarded as a staple part of modern village cricket and is demanded by players as a right.

The Current Era

"In cricket, as in most things, changes are essential for survival,
although not necessarily for the better"

In 2010 the club's 2nd XI reached the final of the Harry Lund Cup before losing to Derby Congs, the first major cup final that the club had reached since the appearance in the Butterley Cup Final in 1965. A total of 52 players appeared for all senior teams during the season with just over half of the players turning out in 10 matches or more. Of those 52 players, 24 had a batting average in double figures but only eight had an average of 25 or better. It was a similar story in the bowling department: 25 players bowled and actually took a wicket for the club but only nine bowlers took 20 or more wickets.

Melbourne 1st XI, c 2000
Rear L-R: Stan Hatton, Mark Rossi, Phil Maddocks, Nick Carter. Steve Price,
Dominic Rafferty, Colin Wakefield, Albert Wood.
Front: Matt Slater, James Thornton, Alex Slater, Andy Potts, Mark Bailey. (27)

Like many clubs nowadays, long gone are the days where the vast majority of players lived and worked in the immediate area. Though many people would prefer that arrangement, it simply isn't practical in the era of modern cricket. In the same way as Derbyshire, when looking for a new fast-bowler, cannot simply look down the nearest mine shaft for the next Les Jackson, clubs have to search far and wide for their playing staff. If anyone 50 years ago had suggested that we would have players travelling from Derby, Nottingham, Northampton and Milton Keynes to play for the club, you would have been certified as insane, without the need for a doctor's referral. You would also have been in for a trip to the asylum in a straitjacket if you had suggested that both local rivals Swarkestone and Ticknall would be employing professionals to play for them. That, however, is the case. In cricket, as in most things, changes are essential for survival, although not necessarily for the better in the eyes of many people.

Player recruitment and retention is paramount to any successful team and, like most other clubs, Melbourne has come to the conclusion that recruitment must start with junior players. By enthusing young players in the game and the club, the next generation of cricketers will become the rock on which the club will prosper and thrive.

Who would have thought that cricket, once a game for the meadow, would now be a major political tool in the jungle of world affairs?

We like to think we still follow the same principles of players who have represented the club in the past. Cricket is one of a very few sports to have its governing principles referred to as laws: most other games and sports have rules or regulations that players have to abide by. The Laws of Cricket were administered firstly by the Marylebone Cricket Club, and now by the International Cricket Council.

As for cricket in the next 150 years, experts would have you believe that it will become 'virtual' cricket, played from your front room, connected to a screen and equipment via the Ethernet. You will need neither equipment, team mates nor even a pitch. Somehow, that image becomes doubtful when set against all that attracts someone to play or watch in the first instance. Besides, where would you go for your post–match pint?

Let's all raise a glass to Melbourne cricket. Long may it continue!

MTCC 2nd XI in the 2010 Harry Lund Cup Final
Rear L-R: Ken Grant, Steve Price, Daniel Marshall, Joe Lacey,
Mathew Heafield, Andy Stanley, Simon Rolfs, Helen Burton (scorer).
Front L-R: Sam Taylor, Dave Potts, Jim Smith (captain),
Vinny Hallifield, Colin Wakefield. (28)

THE ALL TIME GREATEST MELBOURNE XI EVER?

"Loyalty to the club is an asset that is always
particularly appreciated in Melbourne."

Loyalty is a fanciful concept but nevertheless it's a common bar
conversation for football, rugby and cricket teams, both local and national.
Where sport is played, the idea of comparing one generation against
another is a favourite conversation and village cricket is no different.
Melbourne's best ever XI is the opinion of the author and was finalised
from his own memories and those of others spoken to in researching this
book. Cricketing ability apart, the one other overriding factor in selection
was the longevity of cricketing careers at the MTCC. Several players
would have been considered but for the fact that they only played for one
season or a handful of games. Loyalty to the club is an asset that is always
particularly appreciated in Melbourne.

There is an embarrassment of batsmen, wicketkeepers and bowlers
to choose from and a 2nd XI would still have been a fine team. Many
players can consider themselves to be unfortunate not to be included: John
H Young, Fred Bentley, Mark Winters, Dennis Dunnicliffe, Pete Clough,
Vic Jackson, Malcom Spare, Bud Toon, Mick Meakin, Fraser Harrison
and Eric Dunnicliff easily spring to mind. Some of today's juniors may
well go on to establish themselves as Melbourne Legends and when this
book is updated for the 200th anniversary in 2061, watch out for the names
of Price, Potts and Heafield. Players from the late 19th and early 20th
century are at some obvious disadvantage as we have very few records
from those days, let alone anyone's personal memories. I have gone for an
all pace attack but named as 12th man, two spinners who, in modern
parlance, could form part of the squad. The team has also been selected to
represent different generations throughout the club's 150 years of
existence. Three current players appear in the list, one from 1875, two
from the early 1900s, with the others making their debuts between the

1950s and 1990s. More detailed biographies appear in the player directory - see chapter 18.

In batting order, here is Melbourne's 1st XI, 1861 – 2011:

1. Opening the batting at number one is **Roy Grummett**, master batsman of the late 1950s through to the 1990s. His was a prized wicket for any bowler and he was a batsman capable of Boycott-like occupation of the crease, who on many occasions batted through.
2. Roy's batting partner is **J F Andrews**, from the victorious championship side of 1912. Very few records exist of that time but his 107 runs out of a team total of 157 in the championship final against Spondon shows what a fine batsman he must have been.
3. **Mark Rossi** from the current line up comes in at number three: a very stylish batsman who has shown great loyalty to the club when his ball striking power could have taken him to play at a much higher level.
4. From the team that brought cricket back to Melbourne in the 1950s and batting at number four is **Frank Heafield**. At 91 years of age, he is the club's oldest surviving player and still very active. Frank was a powerful batsman and is still a spectator at many games.
5. In at wicketkeeper is the current club Chairman, **Tel Potts**, although he could have conceivably been selected as a bowler. Tel is also Captain of the team and I would expect him to lead from the front in the finest traditions of Melbourne cricket – hard but fair.
6. One of the team all-rounders is **Bas Farmer**. Big hitting Bas would regularly launch six hits into what was then Hatton's Yard and is now Hatton's Court. Before turning out for Melbourne he was a regular for the Breedon side that, prior to Sunday limited overs cricket, would regularly field a team that contained many county players. Surprisingly, Bas wouldn't be opening the bowling or even first change; he would be the team's 'go to' bowler in times of crisis. If playing today, the residents of Hatton's Court would be in great danger.
7. The current 1st XI skipper also comes into the team as an all-rounder and would bowl first change. **Alex Slater** is another who has stayed loyal to the club when his talents could conceivably have taken him elsewhere. His run making at number seven would be an added bonus. He has played for the club since 1988 and been Captain for the past nineteen years.

8. When someone has played for the club for 40 odd years it would be very hard to leave him out of any all-time list. **Colin Wakefield** would be one of my first change bowlers and a very capable batsman. It's estimated that, allowing for 25 matches a year, 'Wakie' has played over 1,000 games for the club.

9. The only known Melbourne cricketer to have played county cricket, **Jim Horsley**, gets in the side with ease and I assume no arguments. When you have played for Nottinghamshire and Derbyshire you should get into Melbourne's all-time XI by right. There is a more detailed biography of Jim in the chapter dedicated to this MTCC legend. Jim would still have a fight on his hands over who would get the new ball.

10. One of the opening bowlers and perhaps, for many, a surprising choice, but in the 1970s **Dick Tivey** bowled with real fire and, like many fast-bowlers, when his confidence was high he would combine hostility with accuracy. He was very capable of running through a side if his Captain had faith in him. Dick had a very long memory and anyone who had bowled short at him even many seasons ago could expect a hearty welcome when coming into bat.

11. The other opening bowler must be **C Randon** who, according to the Derby Mercury, was employed as a professional cricketer by the club in 1875. The only recorded match shows that he bowled 9 overs and took six wickets for 9 runs against a Derby XI on August 18th that year. He sounds like quite a bowler!

12. Twelfth Man, or men in this case: I have chosen two spinners who although they might not be the best ever players to appear for the club have 'Melbourne Cricket' running through their veins. They both played in the late fifties and were still playing regularly throughout the seventies into the eighties. **Stan Hatton** would bowl left-handed off spin from the appropriately named Hatton's Yard end and his nagging line and length would encourage a batsman to take him on. **Lennie Barber**, right handed off spinner would complement him at the other end; he's also chosen for his skills as a groundsman. After all, it's no use assembling the all-time team if they have to play on a cabbage patch.

The team would also need a scorer, umpire and tea lady so step forward Mick Bareham, George Ensor and Mrs Turner respectively. Of course, there could be only one team for Melbourne's greatest XI to play against: bring on the local rivals, Ticknall.

Ticknall C C, 1954, respected local rivals
Rear L-R: Glyn Dakin, Lol Peach, George Minnion, George Harrison,
Harry Minnion, Jack Richards, 'Pen' Hill.
Front L-R: Bob Peach, Charlie Woodward, Sam Stanton,
Albert Decamps, Jack Harrison. (29)

GROUND HISTORY AND
LORD WALTER TALBOT KERR

"Before being made First Naval Lord, the
Professional head of the Royal Navy"

The current ground in Cockshut Lane was given to the people of
Melbourne by Admiral of the Fleet, Lord Walter Talbot Kerr, GB, PC,
who was the British First Naval Lord from 1899 to 1904. (Fig. 30)

To quote from the original Deed of Conveyance dated November 30th 1920, he gave the ground to the inhabitants of Melbourne:

"As an expression of his thankfulness to Almighty God for the victory given to the British Empire and their Allies in the recent European war and for the safe return of his three sons."

Also mentioned in the deed is allowing:

"The said piece of land to be used primarily as a cricket ground and the Melbourne Town Cricket Club ... shall have first but exclusive right to the use of the cricket ground."

"Lord Walter Talbot Kerr was born at Newbattle Abbey, Midlothian, on 28 September 1839, the fourth son of the 7th Marquess of Lothian (1794–1841) and his wife, the former Lady Cecil Talbot (1808–1877). He was educated at Radley College from 1851 to 1853, when he joined the Prince Regent as a naval cadet. During the Baltic operations of the Crimean War (1854–5) he served in the Neptune and Cornwallis and was promoted to Midshipman in August 1855. The next year he was appointed to the frigate Shannon on the China station.

On the outbreak of the Indian mutiny in 1857, the Shannon was ordered to Calcutta, and he landed with most of his ship's company as a naval brigade. He was wounded in an action near Cawnpore, and was given an independent command at the siege and capture of Lucknow. For this service he was specially rated mate for the rest of the Shannon's commission, and in the following year served for a few months in the same rank in the royal yacht Victoria and Albert, and was promoted to Lieutenant in September 1859. In 1860 he was appointed to the Emerald for three years' service in the channel, and in 1864 he went to the Princess Royal, flagship on the East Indies and Cape station, for another three years. He was promoted commander in 1868 and served in the Hercules, channel squadron, until 1871, and afterwards in the Lord Warden, until promotion to Captain in November 1872. While in the Hercules he was awarded the Royal Humane Society's silver medal for jumping overboard from a height of 30 feet into the Tagus to rescue a man who had fallen from the rigging.

During his first eleven years on the Captains' list, four of them on half pay, Kerr's principal commands were as flag-Captain to Sir Beauchamp Seymour (afterwards Lord Alcester) in the channel squadron (1874–7), and in the Mediterranean (1880–81). In September 1880 he was sent by Seymour (who commanded the combined fleet of the five naval powers assembled to enforce, under the terms of the treaty of Berlin, the surrender of Ulcinj to Montenegro by Turkey) on a special mission to Rıza Pasha, the Turkish governor of Albania. He then had a shore appointment as Captain of the Medway steam reserve until 1885, when Lord George Hamilton, on becoming first lord of the Admiralty in Lord Salisbury's Conservative government, appointed him his naval private secretary.

He retained this appointment at the Admiralty until nearly a year after his promotion to Rear Admiral in January 1889. He then hoisted his flag in the Trafalgar, as second in command in the Mediterranean until 1892, when he returned to the Admiralty as fourth naval lord. In November 1893 he became the Second Naval Lord.

Melbourne Hall and Gardens
Lord Walter Talbot Kerr's residence after his retirement. (31)

He was promoted to Vice Admiral in February 1895 and in May he was appointed commander of the channel squadron, with his flag in the Majestic, for two years. In June 1895 he took part with his squadron in the celebration of the opening of the Kiel Canal. He was appointed Aide-de-Camp to Queen Victoria and a member of the Privy Council. In 1899 he was briefly Second Naval Lord again before being made First Naval Lord, the professional head of the Royal Navy. He was promoted Admiral in March 1900 and by a special order in council he was then promoted Admiral of the Fleet in June 1904, until Trafalgar day (21 October) of that year, when Selborne brought Fisher back from Portsmouth to succeed him as First Naval Lord. He remained on half pay until he retired on account of Fage in September 1909. He was President of the Catholic Union of Great Britain from 1917 to 1921. After his retirement he resided at Melbourne Hall, Derby, and died there on 12 May 1927."

The Lothian family have had a long association with Melbourne Town Cricket Club and Lord Walter Kerr's great grandson, Lord Ralph Kerr, is the club's Patron in its Anniversary year. Other family members to have been associated with the club are: Captain Andrew Kerr, Mrs Andrew Kerr and Sir Howard Kerr MVO the Marquis of Lothian.

THE LOTHIAN TROPHY AND LIVING LEGENDS

"When playing against Ticknall, there were
predictable cries of 'traitor' from the spectators"

In 2010, to celebrate the 90th anniversary of the gift of the cricket
ground to the people of Melbourne, Lord Ralph Kerr, great grandson of
Lord Walter Kerr, presented the club with a silver cup inscribed 'The
Lothian Trophy' to be competed for annually between the club's
Development XI and the Melbourne Legends XI – a team consisting of
former players. The first match was played on Sunday June 20th and was
won by the Legends XI, ably captained by Steve Price.

With a crowd of over 200 enjoying the perfect weather and meeting
old friends and cricketing companions, the match was almost of secondary
importance. That is not to say that the game was being taken lightly; runs
and wickets were celebrated as keenly as in any test match. After all, local
pride and bragging rights for the next year were being contested. The
game was a very close affair, batting performances being curtailed by
players retiring if they made 25 runs and other players' contributions
being severely handicapped by their proximity to the beer tent when
fielding or not batting. The youngest player on show was the Development
XI's, eight year old Harry Potts, who took great delight in taking the
wickets of his grandfather, Tel (given out LBW) and father Dave
(bowled). However, Harry's contribution couldn't help his team overcome
the wily Legends team who won by eight runs.

The Legends match is now a part of the club's annual fixtures and
will be played every year on Father's Day thus providing all potential
participants the best ever excuse for playing cricket as surely on Father's
Day each and every male cricketer is allowed to participate. One other fact
from the first Legends match: the beer tent sold out!

With the greatest respect to all those veteran players who appeared
in the match for the Legends XI they still have some way to go before they
meet the true requirements of becoming an MTCC 'legend'. Playing
cricket for the club over many years is the first and obvious requirement

and the other factor is longevity of life. Put the two together and you have a blueprint: someone who played for the club in the 1950s and is by now, likely to have passed 70 years of age. If Melbourne Town Cricket Club had a hall of fame, these living legends would be in it.

With a combined age of nearly 600 years, the Melbourne Legends XI face up to the Development XI in 2010 for the annual challenge match. Lord Ralph Kerr (centre) and to the right, Frank and Fred Heafield. (32)

Frank Heafield is the Club's oldest surviving cricketer who will be celebrating his 91st birthday in our anniversary year and hoping to reach his own personal century in 2020. He was a hard hitting batsman who originated from Ticknall. In the 1959 season when playing against Ticknall there were predictable cries of 'traitor' from the spectators gathered around the boundary. That wasn't too surprising given the local rivalry but the loudest shouts came from his sister, Maggie! He's the elder brother of Fred and was given the nickname of 'Satan' when a boy: draw your own conclusions as to why! He won the club batting trophy in successive seasons, 1953 and 1954. In the latter season he hit a remarkable 22 off the final over to beat Ashby Hastings. Also in the 1954 season he was bowled for a first ball duck when playing against Ockbrook; there was nothing too remarkable in that but the bowler was his 15 year old nephew, Derek Heafield, who went on to take 5 wickets for 11 runs as Melbourne were bowled out for 27. Derek went on to become a cricketing legend at Elvaston Cricket Club. Frank scored 52 against Belper Meadows in the same season. He was also a fine footballer who recalls playing at a pitch at the bottom of Holywell Lane in Kings Newton for Melbourne Young Conservatives. When one of the players broke a leg during the game the ambulance couldn't get to the ground and the other players had to remove a five bar gate from its hinges and carry the player on the gate to the waiting ambulance on Packhorse Road. Frank lived for many years at Mickleover but moved back to Melbourne a few years ago, is now a regular at the Welcome Cafe and still comes to watch the club with his son, Rodney.

MTCC 1st XI, c1956
Rear L-R: Eric Wilson (umpire), Fred Bentley, Pete Clough, Stan Hatton, Richard Hatton, Dennis Dunnicliffe, George Ensor (umpire).
Front L-R: Roy Grummett, Lol Beardsley, Jim Houghton, Leon Tivey (captain), John Turner, Frank Heafield. (33)

Roy Grummett was the 1st XI opening bat for many years, who played in the 1965 Butterley Cup Final. Born in Derby, he moved to Melbourne as a boy and when young worked at Castle Mills before running several businesses locally until retirement. He was a very technically correct batsman and a prized wicket for bowlers. He batted through in many innings and is on everyone's list of the club's top batsmen of all time. He captained the 2nd XI in 1971 and the 1st XI in 1975. Roy was the model of reliability, as witnessed by the 61 runs he made in an opening partnership of 154 with Mark Winters against Sudbury on July 15th 1979; he followed that up with 70 runs the following week against Derby Congs. He first played for the club in the mid 1950s and was still topping the batting averages some 35 years later in the 1990 season. When spotted as a spectator at the 2010 Legends match it was quite conceivable that he could still have put on his pads and batted the afternoon out. Roy still lives in Melbourne; he was 74 on December 16th 2010 and can still occasionally be seen watching cricket.

Opening the batting, early 1960s
Fred Bentley (left) and Roy Grummett. (34)

Dennis Dunnicliffe played in the same 1950s team as Frank Heafield. He was a very dependable opening batsman who also captained the 2nd XI in 1956. As witnessed by his 59 not out against Sandiacre on June 2nd 1955, he was an accumulator of runs, not forgetting that in those days outfields weren't the smoothly manicured surfaces they are now. Many very good shots were restricted to one run as the ball quickly became wrapped up in the high grass on the way to the boundary. Any half century was worth much, much more in today's terms. He lives in Lount and can regularly be seen at his local, the Ferrers Arms.

Lennie Barber was a right arm off spinner and batsman who worked his bowling magic for many years and also made a mighty contribution to the club (and still does) by his work on the ground. Lennie first played in the late 1950s and he played in the 1965 Butterley Cup Final when the club lost to Aitons Welfare at International Combustion ground. He was Captain of the 2nd XI in 1981 and was still turning his arm over in the late 1980s. For many years he worked at the Nixon and Knowles woodyard in Potter Street. Lennie still lives in Melbourne and has always enjoyed long distance walking. In the early 1980s he and some cricket club mates went to watch the West Indians play Derbyshire at Queens Park in Chesterfield. When play started the West Indies still had 3 wickets left of their first innings. Mike Hendrick wrapped that up with a hat trick off the first 3 balls of the day; Derbyshire then batted and were all out for 51 with the West Indies then making their required runs in their second innings and the match finished shortly before 1pm. It was off to the pub for his club mates but Lennie decided to take the opportunity to stretch his legs with a "short" walk of 25 miles around the locality before heading home.

Charles (Fred) Heafield will be 85 in our anniversary year and is the younger brother of Frank. He was an opening bat, wicketkeeper and occasional spinner who captained the 2nd XI in 1961. Like his brother Frank, Fred was originally from Ticknall and is renowned for being the teller of terrible jokes. When opening the batting and walking to the wicket at 2pm he would announce to his club mates that he would be back shortly before tea with a century under his belt; invariably he returned sooner than promised. He would smoke a manikin cigar whilst umpiring and when responding to cries of "howzat?" he would slowly bring his hand up as if to signal out then divert to taking the cigar from his mouth before answering the appeal in the negative and blowing a smoke ring. Like Frank, he was also a good footballer and turned out as a guest player for Crystal Palace reserves whilst doing his national service with the Royal Army Medical Corp at the Royal Herbert Hospital in South East London. Fred still lives in Melbourne, is an active member of the Rotary Club and plays flat green bowls.

Pete Clough was another right arm off spinner and batsman. Even allowing for some exaggeration, Melbourne legend has it that Pete could almost turn the ball at right angles. Pete first played as a youngster in 1954 and continued to play for the next 12 years. He took 7 wickets for 25 runs for the 1st XI against Strodex on August 1st 1955. Pete is an accomplished photographer, a member of the Photographic Society and his pictures have captured Melbourne life for many years. Pete has had several exhibitions; the chances are if you have been to an event in Melbourne in the last 15 years you've probably seen Pete in attendance as he is an official photographer with the Village Voice. He recalls going to a match against Belper Meadows as a passenger in a car driven by that other legend, Fred Heafield and, in those pre-satellite navigation days, following Graham Whyatt and getting hopelessly lost. They finally arrived at 4.45 pm; unfortunately the match started at 3pm but luckily for them they had batted first and unusually there hadn't been a batting collapse.

MELBOURNE? YOU DON'T SOUND AUSTRALIAN!

"We both have our Brads"

Anyone who has ever held a conversation on holiday will undoubtedly have reached a point where they have been asked where they come from. Upon answering "Melbourne", there could be several potential responses, but mainly centring on the fact that you don't sound Australian! It's no use answering that we don't have wallabies where I come from, because we do; in North Derbyshire they are to be found in the wild after escaping from a private zoo in the 1940s. However, there are some differences that you can bring to the attention of your newly found holiday friends.

The Australian Melbourne Cricket Club was founded in 1838, some 23 years before its Derbyshire counterpart and has grown into a much larger club which has hosted numerous test matches. There is one link, albeit a tenuous one: in 1861 when the first games of cricket were being played in Melbourne, Derbyshire, the first English cricket touring party left these shores for Australia and arrived on Christmas Eve. Their tour was hosted by the Melbourne Cricket Club of Australia. Quoting from Alf Batchelder's "Pavilions in the Park, a history of the MCC" (Australia):

"The week after Christmas 1861 was the most exciting the Ground had seen. For three days, the MCG was used for the Caledonian Games, which culminated in football, cavalry exercises and the Coeur de Lion feat, in which horsemen attacked sheep carcases with swords. Then, on New Year's Day 1862, the Eighteen of Melbourne and Districts played H H Stephenson's All-England Eleven".

The Magnificent Seven was a western film starring Yul Brynner, generally held to be the finest of its kind. Here are 7 more comparisons between two magnificent cricket clubs, generally held to be the finest of their kind.

1. In 2009, MCC Australia had 100,280 members; MTCC Derbyshire had an impressive 94.

2. In addition to cricket, MCC Australia is an umbrella organisation for many sports including baseball, bowls (which includes croquet), golf, hockey, lacrosse, real tennis, shooting, squash and tennis. MTCC Derbyshire, unashamedly, plays only one sport, cricket.

3. MCC Australia has four teams that participate in the Victorian Premier Cricket competition and won the Premiership in the season 2009/2010. MTCC Derbyshire plays in the Derbyshire and District League and its 2nd XI reached the Harry Lund Cup Final in 2010.

4. The current ground of the MCC Australia in Yarra Park has held 90,800 spectators when Australia played the West Indies. The ground of the MTCC Derbyshire in Cockshut Lane had almost 200 spectators for the 2010 Legends of Cricket match.

5. The MCC Australia ground was the scene for the infamous underarm ball bowled by Trevor Chappell against New Zealand in 1981 to stop the batsman hitting a 6 off the last ball of the match. No one at the MTCC Derbyshire has deliberately bowled underarm but there have been many instances of the ball almost travelling the full length of the wicket "on the deck".

6. Pope John Paul II and the Reverend Billy Graham appeared at the MCC Australia. Gerald and Kenneth Harcombe, the sons of the local vicar, played for the MTCC Derbyshire.

7. We both have our Brads: Australian legend Donald Bradman played numerous times at the MCC Australia. Alan Bradley, Melbourne legend, played numerous times at the MTCC Derbyshire.

When two worlds collide Melbourne Town club cap from the 1960s, with the kangaroo and ram. (35)

JIM HORSLEY, MTCC LEGEND AND COUNTY CRICKETER

"The only cricketer to play for the MTCC, play county cricket and take a hat trick against Australia"

A young Jim Horsley shows off his classic bowling action . (36)

James (Jim) Horsley was born in Melbourne on January 4th 1890. In the 1891 census, the family is shown as living at 72 Quick Close, Melbourne. John Horsley, Jim's father, is listed in the 1901 census as being an engine driver. John is also shown in the Derby Mercury of May 31st 1893 as playing for Melbourne against Draycott and he also appears in the 1895 batting averages. The family was related to J H Young who played for Derbyshire between 1899 and 1901. Another relation may have been J Horsley who, in 1877, was the umpire for a Derbyshire XI when they played against Yorkshire at Sheffield.

Jim is the only known player to have been born in Melbourne, play for MTCC and go on to play county cricket. In the 1910 season, when aged 20, he is recorded as playing and taking four catches for the MTCC on the scorecard kept by A E Andrews.

He made his first class debut for Nottinghamshire in June 1913 against Yorkshire, when he took two wickets in the first innings, but never had the chance to bat. He managed three no balls and two wides in the match. In his second match against Hampshire he was stumped for a duck, took no wickets, and bowled four wides. He played one more match for Nottinghamshire against Middlesex, when he took a wicket but gave away no extras. However, he had come to the attention of the Derbyshire selectors and in 1914 Jim switched to his native county Derbyshire and played a full prewar season.

He managed 5 five-wicket innings against Somerset, Yorkshire with 6 for 77, Northamptonshire, Leicestershire with a spectacular 6 for 17, and Worcestershire. Against Essex he bowled and in return was bowled by Johnny Douglas and in the Leicestershire match had a match haul of 10 wickets.

Cricket was then interrupted by World War I. Jim, like many patriotic Englishmen, enlisted in the army, firstly with the Nottinghamshire and Derbyshire Sherwood Foresters followed by, in 1917, a transfer to the Royal Flying Corps (RFC) at Farnborough, Hampshire. The RFC was the forerunner of the Royal Air Force (RAF), the RAF being founded on April 1st 1918.

After the war ended (Derbyshire lost six of their players during the war), Jim came back for the 1919 season, and had 3 five-wicket innings, in one of which, he took 6 for 78 against Yorkshire. He then took 6 for 55 and 6 for 62, including a hat-trick, in a match against the Australian Imperial Forces XI, giving him a match total of 12 wickets. This win by 36 runs was the only victory achieved by a county side against the Australians during their tour. The Australian team had a powerful line-up with nearly all the players being international cricketers including Bert

OFFICIAL SCORE CARD.—Corrected to the fall of each wicket.   Price 2d.

COUNTY CRICKET GROUND, DERBY.

JULY 14th and 15th. 1919.   Lunch 1.30.   Stumps Drawn at 7.0

Derbyshire v. Australian I. F.

Bowlers	DERBYSHIRE.	First Innings.		Second Innings.	
1	Mr L Oliver	c Oldfield, b Lampard ..	19	c Oldfield, b Gregory ..	8
2	Cadman	b Gregory	8	b Gregory	8
3	Beet	b Gregory	0	c Stirling, b Collins ..	18
4	Malthouse	c Winning, b Collins ..	30	b Gregory	9
5	Morton	b Lampard	36	b Gregory	1
6	Mr J D Southern	c Oldfield, b Gregory ..	7	c Lampard, b Gregory..	43
7	Revill	b Winning	16	c Winning, b Collins ..	0
8	Wild	st Oldfield, b Trennery	31	c Gregory, b Collins....	2
9	Severn	not out	21	c Gregory, b Collins ..	10
10	Horsley	st Oldfield, b Stirling ..	0	lbw, b Gregory	0
11	Ratcliffe	st Oldfield, b Trennery	8	not out	5
		byes 1 lb 5 wds nb 4	10	byes 2 lb 3 wds nb 3	8

Umpires —
Messrs Mycroft & Shaw   Total 181   Total 112

Fall of Wickets—1st Inns.   2nd Inns.

1	2	3	4	5	6	7	8	9	10	1	2	3	4	5	6	7	8	9	10
26	26	39	81	93	121	125	175	179	181	15	18	42	47	48	50	68	100	106	112

BOWLING ANALYSIS.	Overs	Mdns	Runs	Wkts	Overs	Mdns	Runs	Wkts
Gregory	29	5	75	3	16·3	2	65	6
Collins	16	5	23	1	16	3	39	4
Lampard	17	2	47	2	..	0	..	0
Winning	12	6	15	1	..	0	..	0
Stirling	7	3	6	1	..	0	..	0
Trennery	2·4	1	5	2	..	0	..	0

Batsmen	AUSTRALIAN XI	First Innings.		Second Innings.	
1	Mr H L Collins	c Ratcliffe, b Horsley ..	0	c Ratcliffe, b Horsley ..	16
2	Mr J M Trennery	b Horsley	69	c Beet, b Horsley	9
3	Mr E Ball	c Malthouse, b Morton..	3	lbw, b Morton	5
4	Mr C E Pellew	b Morton	15	b Horsley	0
5	Mr C B Willis	c Horsley, b Morton....	0	b Horsley	1
6	Mr J T Murray	b Horsley	0	b Morton	54
7	Mr A W Lampard	lbw, b Horsley	0	b Horsley	0
8	Mr W S Stirling	lbw, b Horsley	0	b Morton	0
9	Mr J Gregory	b Horsley	28	c Wild, b Horsley	5
10	Mr E A Oldfield	not out	2	not out	26
11	Mr C S Winning	lbw, b Morton	5	st Beet, b Ratcliffe	10
		byes lb 2 wds nb 2	4	byes 2 lb 2 wds nb 2	6

Total 125   Total 132

Fall of Wickets—1st Inns.   2nd Inns.

1	2	3	4	5	6	7	8	9	10	1	2	3	4	5	6	7	8	9	10
0	6	42	42	55	55	55	101	118	125	19	26	26	28	36	41	42	60	105	132

BOWLING ANALYSIS.	Overs	Mdns	Runs	Wkts	Overs	Mdns	Runs	Wkts
Horsley	19	6	55	6	21	6	62	6
Morton	19	6	66	4	22	2	54	3
Ratcliffe	..	0	..	0	1·5	0	10	1
	..	0	..	0	..	0	..	0
	..	0	..	0	..	0	..	0
	..	0	..	0	..	0	..	0

Next Match at Derby—Aug. 4th & 5th (Bank Holiday) v. WARWICKSHIRE.

For Special Report of this Match, see to-day's

DERBY DAILY TELEGRAPH.

Printed on the Ground by "The Sitwell Press," of Back Sitwell St., Derby.

The official scorecard from the match against the touring Australians showing 12 wickets in the match for J Horsley and his hat trick victims, Murray, Lampard and Stirling. (37)

Oldfield, who was acknowledged as the best wicketkeeper in the world at that time, and C E 'Nip' Pellew who went on to score two centuries against England in 1921. Jim was able to capitalise on the absence in the match of Billy Bestwick, who had returned to bowl for Derbyshire that season but was playing for the Players against the Gentlemen at Lords. Jim did not play for the county at all in 1921 and 1922 and went to play in the Lancashire League. During this time he recorded 2 ten-wicket hauls against Forest Wanderers and Burnley.

Jim Horsley, back row, 2nd from the right, taken playing for Derbyshire against Nottinghamshire at the Recreation Ground in Ilkeston in 1925. (38)

In the 1923 season Jim was back with Derbyshire and for the remainder of his career he was sharing the bowling with two of Derbyshire's best bowlers, Bestwick and Arthur Morton. His finest season was 1923 with 7 five-wicket innings and an average of 16.17. He took 7 for 48 in the initial game against Warwickshire, 6 for 29 against

Northamptonshire - a 10 wicket match, 5 for 40 and 5 for 48 in a match against Somerset, 5 for 58 against Glamorgan, 5 for 69 against Yorkshire and 6 for 49 against Leicestershire. In the 1924 season he took 6 for 42 against Yorkshire.

In his last season of 1925 he took 6 for 94 against Gloucestershire, 6 for 66 against Essex and 5 for 36 against Kent. In July that year Jim played in what must have been a poignant match for him against his former county Nottinghamshire that took place at the Rutland Recreation Ground in Ilkeston. The match ended in a draw with Jim bowling 20 overs including 2 maidens that cost 76 runs but took no wickets. The Nottinghamshire team included fast-bowler Harold Larwood, who went on to play for the MCC, and be one of the major players in the world famous test series against Australia in 1932 that will forever be known as the

Big Jim strides to the wicket during his time as club professional at the North of Ireland cricket club. (39)

bodyline tour. Larwood took 76 wickets in the 1925 season and went on to play for England the next year. Jim was a right arm, medium pace bowler taking 267 wickets at an average of 20.26 and a best performance of 7-48 with 19 five-wicket innings and 3 ten-wicket matches. He was a right-hand batsman and played 132 innings in 87 first class matches with an average of 13.67 and a top score of 66. In 1926, he returned to Lancashire League cricket playing for Burnley and then spent two summers as the professional at the Aberdeenshire Cricket Club.

Jim married May Straw in December 1911: she sadly passed away in 1929 and following her death he became the professional for the North of Ireland cricket club in Belfast between 1929 and 1932. His final club in Northern Ireland was the Lisburn cricket and lawn tennis club where he played between 1933 and 1936. Jim spent a total of seven seasons in Northern Ireland and was held in high regard by all those who came into contact with him as can be witnessed by the testimonial letters written by the club secretaries during this period. They describe him as "a capable batsman", "match winning bowler", "capable coach", "a cricketer of high standard", "a gentleman" and finally "at all times, honest, trustworthy and sober".

In his career, Jim played at all the major test grounds of that era: Trent Bridge both for and against Nottinghamshire, against Warwickshire at Edgbaston in Birmingham, against Lancashire at Old Trafford in Manchester, against Yorkshire at Headingley in Leeds, against Surrey at the Oval and against Middlesex at Lords, both in London.

He also played against many of the giants of the game during his playing career including:

Maurice Leyland (Yorkshire) played forty one test matches between 1928 and 1938 proving himself one of the best left-handers of his generation. He made 2,764 runs for England at 46.06 with 9 hundreds and 10 fifties, with a highest score of 187.

Wilfred Rhodes (Yorkshire) played fifty eight test matches for England between 1899 and 1930. In those matches, Rhodes took 127 wickets and scored 2,325 runs, becoming the first Englishman to complete the double of 1,000 runs and 100 wickets in test matches. He holds the world records both for the most appearances made in first-class cricket (1,110 matches), and for the most wickets taken (4,204).

Herbert Sutcliffe (Yorkshire) was an English professional cricketer who represented Yorkshire and England as an opening batsman. Apart from one match in 1945, his first-class career spanned the period between the two World Wars. Sutcliffe played in fifty four test matches for England and on three occasions he toured Australia, where he enjoyed outstanding success. His last tour in 1932–33 included the controversial "bodyline" series.

Joe Hardstaff (Nottinghamshire) was a central figure in the Nottinghamshire side until he retired at the end of the 1924 season. Having helped his county to its first County Championship in 1907, he was picked for the MCC tour to Australia in 1907/08, captained by the Nottinghamshire county captain Arthur Jones. Hardstaff was a big success on the tour, scoring more runs in first-class matches than any other batsman.

Patsy Hendren (Middlesex) was one of the most prolific English batsmen of the period between the wars, averaging 47.63 in his fifty one tests. He has the third highest first class run aggregate of 57,611 runs (after Sir Jack Hobbs and Frank Woolley), and his total of one hundred and seventy centuries ranks second only to Hobbs, who played with him many times and called him "a great cricketer and great companion".

Harry Storer (Derbyshire) was a right-handed batsman, leg spin bowler and occasional wicketkeeper. He played in more than three hundred first-class matches between 1920 and 1936, all of which were for Derbyshire. In his last season, he helped Derbyshire to win their only County Championship. He is better known for playing and managing Derby County Football Club and won two international football caps for England.

In retirement Jim ran several pubs in the Derby area including the Duke of Devonshire in Goodwin Street, the Hare and Hounds in Erasmus Street and the Shakepeare Inn in Sadler Gate. He never needed much prompting from the regulars to explain how he bowled out the Australians

in 1919 and was proud to show the mounted ball from that match, which always took pride of place amongst the souvenirs of his cricket career. In the 1960s, Jim paid an emotional return visit to his first cricket club, the MTCC, as the honoured guest at the club dinner. He attended the Derbyshire centenary dinner in 1970 and was made an honorary life member of the county. In retirement, Jim lived in the Derwent flats in Nottingham Road, overlooking the County ground at Derby. Jim died in Derby on February 13th 1976 at the age of eighty six.

In retirement, Jim was always proud to show the hat trick ball from 1919. (40)

MELBOURNE PLAYERS WHO PLAYED FIRST CLASS CRICKET

"Played against the West Indies in 1966 and
in the following season, for Melbourne"

A total of four people who were born in Melbourne have played first class cricket (so far!) and they are all included below. However, there is no proven link between them and the Melbourne Town Cricket Club. Additionally, two others have played first class cricket prior to playing for the club.

George Burrill Earl (August 7th 1859 - April 20th 1933) was born, lived, worked and died in Melbourne. He was registered with Derbyshire between 1883 and 1888 but played in only one first class county game where he was out for four runs and took one catch for Derbyshire against the MCC on July 9th 1883. He was a right handed bat and right arm fast medium bowler. In the census of 1901 he was listed as an innkeeper with his wife, Mary and 3 children living in Castle Street. The inn in question may have been either the White Swan or the Castle Inn. There is a G Earl listed in the Derby Mercury archives as being top of the 1st XI batting averages for Melbourne in 1896. George Burrill Earl would have been 37 at that point; it could have been the same person.

Guy Denis Wilson (November 30th 1882 - November 30th 1917) was in born in Melbourne and played for Derbyshire in 1902 and 1905. He played one first class match for Derbyshire in 1902 against W G Grace's London County but made little impact in the match. W G himself opened the batting for London. His second game came three years later against MCC when again he made little impression. He played four innings in two first class matches with an average of 4.75 and a top score of 9. He took no wickets in the six overs he bowled. Wilson saw service in World War I and was killed in France on his 35th birthday during the Battle of

Cambrai. In that battle, the British lost over 44,000 men and the Germans 45,000.

John Henry Young (2 July 1876 - 2 August 1913) was born in Melbourne, the son of Mark Young, a joiner, and his wife Emily. He played for Derbyshire between 1899 and 1901.

In the 1895 season at the age of 19, a John Young is shown in the MTCC club averages printed in the Derby Mercury of October 2nd. He took 63 wickets for 354 runs to finish with an average of 5.41. He also batted in 15 innings, scoring 90 runs at an average of 6.42. In 1896 he took 4 wickets playing against Woodville. It is possible that it is the same John Young.

Young made his debut for Derbyshire in the 1899 season, in June, against Yorkshire, when he made a duck in both innings and took no wickets in a short spell of bowling. He played three matches in the season and made his top-score of 42 not out against Worcestershire in his final match that year.

Young played more regularly throughout the 1900 season, and matched his previous season's high against Leicestershire. He also gained his best bowling figures of 5 for 65 against London County, and took four wickets against Nottinghamshire. In the 1901 season he played more matches than in any other season, but his batting and bowling performances failed to match those in previous seasons.

Young was a right-arm medium-fast-bowler and took 28 first class wickets at an average of 35.57 and with a best performance of 5 for 65. He was a right handed batsman and played 48 innings in 28 first class matches with an average of 9.71 and a top score of 42 not out.

One of his Derbyshire team-mates during the 1901 season was Charles Augustus Ollivierre, the first black West Indian cricketer to play for an English county, who played for Derbyshire between 1901 and 1907. Young died in Melbourne at the age of 37 and was related to Jim Horsley, who also played for Derbyshire.

Norton Montresor Hughes-Hallett (18 April 1895 - 26 March 1985) was born in Melbourne, and was the son of Norton Joseph Hughes-Hallett, who played several games for Leicestershire, including a match against the Australian tourists in 1880, and his wife Alice Louisa Denton. He was educated at Haileybury College. He made his debut for Derbyshire in August 1913 in a match against Lancashire when he scored 32 in the first innings and took a wicket. He made little impact in the remaining two games that season. He played three games in 1914 with his top score of 67 against Hampshire and 53 against Leicestershire, but bowled little. In the match against Leicestershire he batted with Melbourne born, MTCC cricketer, Jim Horsley. Hughes-Hallett was an upper-middle order right-hand batsman and played 11 innings in six first class matches for Derbyshire with a top score of 67 and an average of 17.80. He was a leg-break bowler and took one wicket with an average of 27.

Hughes-Hallett served with the King's Shropshire Light Infantry in World War I in France and Belgium and was wounded in action. After the war he served in Ireland from 1919 to 1922. He played several games for the Gentlemen of Shropshire in the Netherlands in 1924. He was then posted to India where he played for the Europeans in two Bombay Quadrangular Tournaments in 1925/26 and 1926/27. He achieved his best bowling performance of 8-81 against the Muslims in 1925/26, but in both years the Europeans lost to the Hindus in the final. In India Hughes-Hallett played six innings in four matches with a top score of 41 and an average of 12.83. However, he took 16 wickets with an average of 17.81 and a best performance of 8-81.

He was a lieutenant-colonel in World War II with British Forces in Curacao from 1941 to 1942 and garrison commander in Barbados in 1945 and 1946. Hughes-Hallet died at Tewkesbury, Gloucestershire at the age of 89. His brother in law was John Pawle, who played for Cambridge University and Essex, between 1935 and 1938.

R E J (Bob) Chambers. (19 November 1943) In 1966, Bob played first class cricket for Cambridge University and, in the following season, a slightly lower class of cricket for Melbourne Town Cricket Club. In 1962 he appeared at the home of cricket, the famous Lord's ground, for the Public Schools against the Combined Services. He played a total of 12 matches for the University in 1966 including games against Warwickshire, Essex, Yorkshire, Somerset, Glamorgan, Sussex and Gloucestershire. As an opening batsman he played against many famous players of that era including Fred Trueman, Geoff Boycott, Brian Close, Dennis Amiss and Basil D'Oliveira. He made three half centuries against Glamorgan, Somerset and Warwickshire; his highest first class score was 58 and he finished with a batting average of 17.54. Against the touring West Indies side in 1966, he played against the world's most famous all-rounder Gary Sobers (who caught and bowled him for 16 in the first innings) and the feared fast-bowler Wes Hall who was bowling off a forty yard run up. Bob gained his university blue playing against Oxford University at Lord's in 1966.

It must have been quite a contrast, changing at Fenners, the home of Cambridge University cricket, in the footsteps of Douglas Jardine and Ted Dexter and the following season changing at Cockshut Lane the home of Melbourne cricket in the footsteps of the Hattons, the Andrews and the Tiveys. Bob was teaching at Foremark Hall at the time and was introduced to the club by Derek Hoare, a leading member of the 1st XI and head teacher at the school. Bob went on to play minor counties cricket for Staffordshire in 1969 and Hertfordshire between 1972 and 1974. Bob, now living near Shrewsbury, picks up the story,

R E J (Bob) Chambers, middle row, second from the right with the
West Indies and Cambridge University teams in 1966
In the front row, far left, is future England captain Mike Brearley. Also on the
front row are Gary Sobers, Rohan Kanhai, Deryk Murray and Wes Hall.
To the right of Bob is David Acfield who went on to play for Essex. (41)

"I am now retired from the teaching profession, where I finished as a Headmaster. Unfortunately, when I was 34 I had an accident where I suffered a fractured skull, and am now a qualified epileptic. Since then, I played very little cricket, but when I did, I represented Wanstead in the Essex League, Frome in the Somerset League, and my local village team, Rode, which supported Real Ale. I am now a qualified Cricket coach Grade 2, and have recently moved to Shropshire to be near my family in Shrewsbury.

When playing seriously, I represented Staffordshire once and Hertfordshire regularly for three years while working at Bishop's Stortford College. I played once for Quidnuncs Cricket Club (whose membership is open to all living Cambridge blues) against the Royal Navy. I drank too much in a submarine, and cannot recall anything of the match at all. I have now joined Worcestershire as a member as I like looking at cathedrals and it is a good ground to see the game. To summarise: I have been a good club cricketer, sound Minor Counties batsman, but only a No. 6 in the 1st Class game, not an opener, as was needed at Cambridge in 1966 when I faced the fiery Wes Hall."

Tony Borrington (8 December 1948). Tony played for the club in 1983. He was born in Spondon and played for Derbyshire 2nd XI in 1965 aged only 17. His first class debut was in 1971 and he played for the county until 1980. He was a right hand batsman, leg break bowler and occasional wicketkeeper. He played 122 first class matches for Derbyshire and had a batting average of 23.63. He is the deputy head teacher at Grace Dieu School at Thringstone near Coalville. His son, Paul, plays for Derbyshire. When playing for Melbourne he had a top score of 60 not out against a League Representative XI on July 26th 1983.

CLUB CHARACTERS AND THEIR STORIES

"But don't forget that I've just turned 90"

In the misty eyes of the romantics, cricket anywhere means mown grass, the smell of linseed oil, cucumber sandwiches and sponge cake, blue skies and the click-click of studded boots on the well-worn pavilion steps, all conjuring images of cricket in the past.

However, when Melbourne cricketers of all generations and abilities get together they don't talk about the best cricketers of past generations or linseed oiled bats, they reminisce about some of the larger than life characters that have played in the past. Here are some of the anecdotes (possibly apocryphal) that have been passed down.

A Melbourne fast-bowler of the 1960s was once staying with a friend in the West Country, and visited a village cricket match on the Saturday afternoon. The visiting side were one short and he was pressed to play without anyone knowing who he was. As both umpires came from the home side, who were batting, it proved difficult to get them out.

In desperation, the Captain asked the Melbourne man if he could bowl. He said that he would have a try and, taking a short run, sent down an off-spinner, which the batsman missed. It hit him in the middle of both legs, which were right in front of the wicket. All the team appealed but "Not out" was the reply.

The next one, a leg-break, was snicked into the wicketkeeper's hands.

Again "Not out" was the reply.

Our man then took his usual run of over twenty yards and sent down a thunderbolt, which knocked all three stumps out of the ground.

Turning to the umpire, he said, "We very nearly had him that time, didn't we?"

A large batsman of the 70s looked as if he had been poured into his cricket whites and had forgotten to say "When!" His figure raised a few eyebrows when he first joined the club. They sent him on a run round the boundary with the rest of the team, but he was just not built to run a long way. After one lap the others had left him behind.

On another occasion, his Captain, before a match, suggested that he should try to do something about his weight.

"Why don't you drink halves instead of pints?" the skipper asked.

After the match and to test his resolve, the Captain asked what he wanted to drink.

Quick as a flash he said, "Two halves, please, skipper!"

At the recent Legends match, one of the older cricketers and an exceptional batsman from the 1950s, was asked how he thought he would have fared against today's bowlers.

He pondered the point for a moment, and then replied, "I think I might have averaged about thirty-eight or thirty-nine perhaps."

The questioner was shaken.

"Surely with all your skill you would have achieved much more than that?"

"Maybe," he said, "but don't forget that I've just turned 90!"

At one time in the 1960s, the club had a great fast bowler who hadn't quite masterminded the other side of cricket, namely batting and, more to the point, running between the wickets.

Playing in an end of season game and batting at number eleven, he got injured and called for a runner. Horrendously, in the next over his batting partner at the other end was also injured and he too called for a runner.

Our man pushed forward and called for a run, forgot that he had a runner and set off himself.

Adding to the unfortunate circumstances was the fact that the other batsman on hearing "run" had also set off at the same time as his runner. In the ensuing melee, someone decided that a second run was on. Due to the confusion and shouts of "yes", "no", "maybe" and "waiting", all four ended up at the same end. One of the fielders smartly picked up the ball and broke the wicket.

The umpire, trying manfully to keep a straight face, brought his finger up and said: "One of you four is out: I don't particularly care which one; just decide and let the scorer know".

THE ART OF MELBOURNE CAPTAINCY AND THOSE WHO HAVE SERVED

"Pick your best XI and then ask the worst player to be the skipper"

Think of skippers and you might think of Captain Sensible, Scott, Scarlet, Bird's Eye, Kirk, or even Cook. None of them ever captained a village cricket team and with good reason; they had far more sense and a day job.

Melbourne cricket Captains have a thankless task, keeping eleven (sometimes less) players all happy, making sure they all bowl, bat and are involved in the field of play. They have to listen to their well meaning advice and then make up their own mind whilst making the players believe they've actually followed their cricketing thoughts.

Captaincy makes a huge impression at any level of the game. A good Captain can make a poor team good and a good team great. If you are ever lucky enough to be Captain of a great team, then relax and enjoy yourself – you've probably died in your sleep and are in cricket heaven.

Cricket is a unique sport: its individual disciplines of bowling, batting and fielding have to be blended into a team structure and, what do you know, it's the Captain's unacknowledged task to do this. It is an assignment not unlike that ancient bar room sport of spoof drinking by taking a maximum of three different drinks, two alcoholic, into a pint glass, then downing them in one swift gulp and trying to keep the concoction down. Anyway, how many really good England Captains can you name against how many really unsuitable bad ones? Never forget, it's not always the best players either who make the best Captains. Who was the best England Captain between Ian Botham, Freddie Flintoff and Mike Brearley and who was the worst player? Maybe that's the way forward; pick your best XI and then ask the worst player to be the skipper, leaving the superstars to concentrate on their own game? MTCC Annual General Meetings take note!

There is a belief and quasi religion known as the Twenty Three Enigma, where all events and incidents are related to the number 23. It was made into a film starring Jim Carrey, a Canadian who, it has to be said, never captained a cricket team. For trivia buffs everywhere, it's also the lowest number you can't score on a dart board with one dart. However, for budding Captains of Melbourne, here are 23 rules to follow. Read through them carefully and, if you still want to be Captain, have yourself declared clinically insane before starting divorce proceedings. Incidentally, this is what happened to Jim Carrey in the film, before he went on to murder his wife!

1.   Make sure you have eleven players on the field at the start of play! You can never take anything for granted. Fourteen players on a Thursday night can quickly turn into nine on Saturday morning.

2.   Give priority in selection to those who come to nets and turn up religiously to matches. If players are rewarded for doing the right thing, they'll do it more often. Always chose youth over age in close selection calls.

3.   Know what you'll do if you win the toss. Think about the conditions, the points system, the relative strength of your team, how much sleep they may have had and how hungover they are. If in doubt, then go with your team's strength; if you've lots of good bowlers, then bowl first. If you all bat, then bat first. Once you're on top, you'll probably win. Of course, first of all you have to win the toss; a good pointer at home is to always have a coin with you. Home Captains have been known to greet the opposition Captain, enquire after his wife, family and team, then arrive in the middle without a coin.

4.   Bowlers bowl better with attacking fields. Always attack the new batsman. If a batsman hits two similar shots into the same place, then put a fielder there. Better still, put a fielder there before he hits the shots. The words 'horse', 'stable door' and 'bolted' spring to mind. Always have a plan or, better still, look like you have one. Looks are deceptive: think of the bespectacled David Steel against the West Indies. Never keep the same field for two different batsmen. Be active!

5. Have a team plan when batting. Yes they really do exist and they make a difference. A team plan should consist of more than which pub we are meeting in before the match. Failing to prepare is preparing to fail and never forget the 6 Ps: Prior Presentation & Preparation Presents Poor Performance. Yes, I know there is a seventh P; work it out for yourself.

6. Serious catching practice and throwing makes a difference. Catches really do win matches. No one means to drop a catch, so encourage everyone to go for everything and praise everyone for every genuine attempt. Keen fielding teams win most of their games.

7. Lead from the front, and make sure your whites are clean and pressed before a game and impress upon your team the same attitude. For the juniors and most of the married men, this will mean looking after your mother or wife and making them feel a part of the cricket environment.

8. We all forget that we were once young and unless our name was Botham, we were very nervous when playing with the big boys. Always make youngsters feel important and give them something to do. If they can't bat or field well, then put them at cover and tell them they're the most important fielder in the side.

9. Don't let anyone but yourself move a fielder to another position. A bowler can move a fielder a few yards but should go through you to move him completely. After having a six hit that went 20 yards over the fielder's head and on to the next pitch, the bowler swapped the boundary fielder with the words "he's better on the boundary than you". "Not twenty yards in the air, he isn't," replied the fielder. Having eleven Captains on the field is a recipe for chaos and arguments.

10. A group jog around the field before play is the best warm up and builds team spirit while intimidating the rag tag, smoking, opposition. Make sure the rag tags aren't in your team.

11. Put your best fielder at first slip, not the worst.

12. Find a good dynamic wicketkeeper and encourage him to stand up to medium pacers. Give everyone a role in the side and make them feel important, and then let them get on with it. Encourage everyone to express themselves - spinners to toss it up, pacemen to bowl fast, stroke makers to hit it and stone wallers to rotate the strike without getting out. Give everyone a job outside the game and make sure they do it. Nothing breeds resentment more than half

the team doing all the setting up or tidying up when the others have already left for the pub.

13. Everyone likes a pat on the back. Praise in public and tell off in private. If someone ignores a warning about their actions, then drop them. You're better off without the prima donna.

14. Sweet talk the umpires. Call them 'sir'. Find out what their hobbies are, make a note and ask next time you see them. The umpire is your friend. It can't do any harm in those close LBW calls. Never, ever, argue with the umpire. You might think he has forgotten what you said but, rest assured, the next time he umpires your match and a close call comes, you'll realise he hasn't forgotten anything.

15. Field at mid-on or mid-off. You can see how the bowler is doing: talk to him before or after an over and control the game. Fielding at slip takes too much concentration and you want to be the one to give the bowler the ball before he unleashes hell.

16. Work harder at nets than anyone else. Arrive first and leave last at games. Lead by example.

17. Make every effort to get a result on wet days. Get the team to help the groundsman as teams with no abandoned games will always finish above teams with three abandoned games.

18. Cricket has a rich tradition of post match socialising. Team-mates, opponents and umpires get together after the day's play to relax, rehydrate, talk about the day's play and reminisce about past exploits. Encourage all players to participate in this part of the game. Many lifelong friendships are formed – both within your team, with spectators and even opponents and umpires. Involve yourself enthusiastically in this sharing of knowledge and debriefing. Your cricket will be the richer for it.

19. Don't talk to bowlers during their over. If they're hooked for four they know to pitch the ball up; they don't need to be told. Don't distract them; trust them, then have a word between overs.

20. Don't sledge or allow sledging. No one wants to play for unpleasant cricket teams.

21. If a bowler is on the point of boiling over, then take him off and let him cool down at long leg. In any dispute over a decision, you must always take the umpire's side. Your job is to keep your team in check and playing in the spirit of the game. You'll be respected more for being cool and calm when everyone else is losing their head. Do the right thing. Don't appeal if you know it's not out.

Don't claim bump balls as catches. Recall a batsman who's been wrongly dismissed. Always occupy the moral high ground. Everyone takes their cue from your behaviour. The game is bigger and more important than this match.

22.   Always be calm and optimistic. If you don't think you're going to win, then you've already lost.

23.   Don't expect anyone to appreciate your efforts. You will thank a hundred people before getting any thanks yourself. You know if you're doing a good job, but don't expect thanks from anyone else. You'll get blamed for everything that goes wrong though; just accept it. Never yell or get angry at team members.

Finally, if you are still resolved to put yourself to the test and stand as Captain, as one Melbourne opener used to say when calling for a quick single, "Good Luck!"

Melbourne Town 1st XI, 1966
Rear L-R: Sergeant Bentley, Tony Gee, John Hallifield, Richard Hatton,
Maurice Harvey, David Calvert, Stan Hatton, Frank Ashmore.
Front L-R: Harold Hodgkinson, Harry Calvert, John Turner, Fred Bentley,
Roy Grummett. (42)

For some it was only for a few matches, some a season, and others longer, however, the following are some of the illustrious people who have Captained one of the club's teams:-

1st XI

W Briggs (1892), W A Newbold (1904), J Wilson (1905), M E Salsbury (1908), Jas W Salsbury (1920), A C Goodband (1921), Arthur E Andrews (1928,), W Barrett (1933), F B Hunt (1939), A Dickman (1952), L Tivey (1956), F Bentley (1958), J Turner (1966), R Grummett (1975), T Potts (1980), C Wakefield (1981), M Bailey (1990) and A Slater (1998).

2nd XI

A J Hatton (1908), E Ensor (1909), A Collyer (1910), J Wilson (1921), W Barrett (1928), F Smith (1929), H Blackburn (1932), A Foddy (1933), C Lane (1936), F Dunnicliffe (1937), G Shaw (1939), L Tivey (1952), C Clayton (1954), D Dunnicliffe (1956), H Hodgkinson (1957), J Turner (1964), A Staniforth (1965), H Calvert (1970), R Grummett (1971), J Dando (1973), T Potts (1974), R Marshall (1975), R Lakin (1976), L Barber (1981), J Hallifield (1990), J Smith (2009) and K Grant (2010).

Sunday XI

J Dando (1976), S Pegg (1977), J Hallifield (1978), A Crowson (1979), R Hatton (1980), M Starkie (1981), A Bradley (1982), M Preston (1991), D Potts (1992), C Lancaster (2009) and A Heafield (2010).

Many of the Captains skippered for more than one season; in all instances the year shown in brackets is the first recorded instance of them doing so. Finally, to quote from the 'Spirit of Cricket', the preamble to the MCC Laws of cricket, written by former England Captains Ted Dexter and Colin Cowdrey:

"Cricket is a game that owes much of its unique appeal to the fact that it should be played not only within its Laws but also within the Spirit of the Game. Any action which is seen to abuse this spirit causes injury to the game itself. The major responsibility for ensuring the spirit of fair play rests with the Captains."

Let's leave it at that.

CLUB ARCHIVES

"Sir Vauncey shunned many modern trappings"

These days, with a click of the mouse, you can see your average, how many games you played, who against and much more. Thanks to the archives of the late Richard Hatton, MTCC records exist going back to the early 20th century.

Going through past score cards is a fascinating look through a social archive of the times. The club not only played against other villages but also teams from long forgotten industries, trades and names that include Worthington's, Ind Coope and Co, Bemrose and Sons, Leys, Belper Potteries, Chaddesden Works, Derby YMCA, Derby Post Office, Midland Hotel, Ashby Hydroleine, Midland Loco, Great Northern, Midland Motive Power, Moira Colliery, Derby Butchers, Truman and Co, New Lount Colliery, Derby LMS, Allsopp and Co, Nadin and Co, Mansfields Limited, LMS Erectors, Strodex, Derby Savings Bank, Derby Cables, Sharp Control Gear Limited, Aitons Welfare, International Combustion, GIC and the Willington Power Station.

It is doubtful if some of the teams we played are still in existence. Who can recall Old Normanton, Handysides, Brook Street SS, Nottingham Forest Wanderers or Ilkeston Conservatives? There was also a fair sprinkling of church based teams including Saint Augustine's, Saint Peter's, Saint Luke's and Saint Michael's. There was even a cricket team from nearby Staunton Harold. In 1957, with a then population of under 100, you assume that every able-bodied man must have been co-opted to play for the team.

Some of the teams we first played many years ago we still play against or they play at a different level of cricket within our league structure: Denby (1910), Allestree (1911), Ockbrook and Borrowash (1921), Alvaston & Boulton (1923), Castle Donington (1937), Ticknall (1951), Swarkestone (1951), Elvaston (1958), Winshill (1972), Rosehill Methodists (1978) and Derby Congregationalists (1978). The first recorded matches are in brackets.

The good, great and mighty have been associated with the club as Vice Presidents and Patrons. It appears that if you were the local doctor, justice of the peace or the local vicar, you were expected to take your place on the governing body of the cricket club, alongside the then pillars of South Derbyshire society. Some notable names associated with the club include:

Sir Vauncey Harpur Crewe of Calke Abbey served as High Sheriff of Derbyshire in 1900 but apart from this position he played little or no part in public life; however, he is listed as being a Vice President of MTCC in the early 20th century. Interestingly, our near rivals, Ticknall Cricket Club, played in Calke Park at one point before moving to their current ground at the Grange in 1922. His communications with his children could be extremely strained, so much so that it was not uncommon for him to communicate with them by letter, delivered by a footman. He was seen as particularly tyrannical toward his daughters. One of his daughters, Airmyne, was banished from Calke Abbey for smoking a cigarette - a ban imposed on his entire household for fear of fire. She never returned to Calke during his lifetime. Sir Vauncey shunned many modern trappings - motor cars and even bicycles were banned on the estate (he preferred to rely on the horse and carriage), electricity was not installed even in his daughters' lifetime, and only after his death was the ancient plumbing system replaced. A possible explanation for this intense dislike of the modern world is that Sir Vauncey had been privately educated at Calke in his youth, and did not attend school or university.

Major J F D Halstead, Captain Drott, Major General M G Taylor, Colonel A S Mainwaring and Major Dawson were all retired army officers who lived locally.

The Right Honourable Earl Cowper was a major landowner of the late 19th and early 20th century.

The Reverends Canon Singleton, C V Raynor and J Daintree were local priests.

Dr A S Tredinnick, Dr A W P Haine, Dr Bruce, Dr A E Ainscow and Dr H Boardman were all local doctors who served the town.

R W Loake JP, W Briggs JP, W Saunders JP and J Bell JP were all prominent citizens who also served as justices of the peace.

Captain Andrew Kerr and Mrs Andrew Kerr were the grandparents of Lord Ralph Kerr who came to live at Melbourne Hall in 1928.

Sir Howard Kerr, MVO was Mrs Andrew Kerr's brother. He was actually the 5th cousin of Mrs Kerr's husband Captain Andrew, which is why they share the same surname. Sir Howard and his wife, Lady Christina, lived at The Dower House in Melbourne.

Sir Herbert H Raphael MP was the Liberal MP for South Derbyshire between 1906 and 1918, who was a barrister, a politician, an art collector and trustee of the (British) National Portrait Gallery. He was one of the oldest soldiers serving in the Great War. In 1915, aged 56, he held the rank of Major with the King's Royal Rifle Corps.

Alderman John Gillies Shields JP was a major land owner who will be forever associated with the Donington race track and Hall.

Sir James Augustus Grant MP was the conservative MP for South Derbyshire between 1924 and 1929.

Lieutenant Colonel Sir Cecil Paget, CMG and DSO, was a British locomotive engineer and railway administrator. In 1906 Cecil Paget married Lady Alexandra Osborne, fourth daughter of the 9th Duke of Leeds, and they restored the 17th century Kings Newton Hall. He served in France with the Railway Operating Division in World War I, commanding operations in France and Belgium and rising to the rank of Lieutenant-Colonel in the Royal Engineers. His military awards were the DSO in 1916, the CMG in 1918 and he was mentioned in despatches. The French awarded him Officier de la Légion d'honneur and the Belgians their Officier de l'Ordre de la Couronne.

Fortunately, nowadays, all sorts of records exist and looking through the website archives of the Derbyshire Leagues from 2004 to the current date, the following Melbourne performances stand out:

- On July 22nd 2007, Alex Slater took 7 wickets for 8 runs when bowling for the 1st XI against Rosehill Methodists in Division 4 South.

- On July 23rd 2007, Russell Allaway scored 152 not out, batting for the 2nd XI against Ticknall 4th XI in Division 7 South.

- On June 20th 2009, Mark Rossi scored 151 not out, batting for the 1st XI against Ashbourne 1st XI in Division 5 South.

- On July 11th 2009, Phil Stanhope took 7 wickets for 16 runs when bowling for the 2nd XI against Castle Donington 2nd XI in Division 10 South.

- On May 23rd 2010, 14 year old Mathew Heafield scored 79 not out, batting for the 2nd XI against Ticknall 4th XI in Division 9 South and took 2 wickets in the same match.

- In the season 2010, Ken Grant took a total of 30 wickets whilst keeping wicket (24 catches and 6 stumpings) and scored 976 runs.

In the entire club archives and records there is one outstanding fact: no female cricketer has ever played for the club. With the starting up of women's cricket in 2011, that fact is destined to become a part of history in the very near future. Stand by for much turning in graves!

THE CLASSIC MELBOURNE NUMBER ELEVEN

"Cards will always have naked women on them"

Melbourne Town 2nd XI, 1978
Players include Lennie Barber, Jonathan Heath, Ray Lakin, Robert Marshall,
Keith Pearce, Stuart Pegg, Steve Taylor and Graham Twells. A classic line up
with veterans, youngsters, club stalwarts and the number eleven missing! (43)

Every now and then, or more often in our case, you come across a cricketer who is somewhat different from the rest of the team, easily identifiable by his dress, manner and ability (or lack of it). Yet, he will get a game because, as is the way with cricket, someone will drop out every week, be getting married, be on holiday or just plain "can't be bothered".

Catch-22 is a book by Joseph Heller, later turned into a film. Catch-22 does not actually exist, but because the powers that be claim it does, and the world believes it does, it nevertheless has potent effects. Indeed, because it does not exist there is no way it can be repealed, undone, overthrown, or denounced. If that description sounds somewhat bizarre and bordering the farcical, that very same description could be applied to many Melbourne number elevens. Unlike Catch-22, the following 22 attributes have existed, and belonged, to various Melbourne number elevens over the years; sadly not all of them belonged to the same player. He would have been a sight to behold.

1. Plays in black trainers.
2. Wears a replica England shirt as part of his whites.
3. Has a Melbourne nickname that is part legend or animal like 'The Badger' or 'Killer'.
4. When excited, usually when talking about his cricket, he talks as he drinks and sprays his beer everywhere.
5. Smokes a cigarette while doing square leg umpiring duties.
6. Shouts 'in' at the end of every run.
7. During practice, wears batting pads to keep wicket.
8. Plays in tracksuit trousers.
9. Wears chinos as that is the closest thing he has to whites.
10. Misses the ball after an almighty heave then walks over to square leg to practise a forward defensive; next ball another heave and another practise of the forward defensive. This is repeated until he is out.
11. Wears a black belt round his trousers.
12. Instead of a belt, has a tie holding his flannels up.
13. Plays in a Fred Perry tennis shirt.
14. Has the most ludicrous windmill bowling action coming close to throwing but can never understand why he doesn't get a bowl and insists on giving coaching advice to young players.
15. Plays in two left-handed gloves.
16. Always borrows playing kit.
17. Batting average of less than one, but will insist on giving coaching advice to young players.
18. Cannot catch a ball and throws it like putting the shot and, yes, likes giving fielding advice to younger players.
19. Never has any money for match subs but can mysteriously finance his post match drinking, which invariably finishes with a curry and taxi ride home.
20. Will insist on regaling the opposition Captain with exploits of his cricketing career.
21. Will always have playing cards ready for when rain stops play. Cards will always have naked women on them.
22. Plays in black socks and wears Y-fronts with messages on them.

CRICKET RELATIONS

"He couldn't possibly give the batsman out, as he was his nephew"

Where would village cricket be without the input of families? Village cricket in Melbourne has always been a family affair, from the great cricketing families of the 1920s – the Tiveys and Andrews through the Hattons and Dunnicliffes of the 1950s right up to the modern day era of the Potts family. In some decades, the committee, groundsman, scorers, tea ladies, umpires and players have been drawn from a seemingly endless supply of volunteers from the surnames of some of Melbourne's well known families. Fathers take their sons to watch them play and invariably the son ends up the better player, much to the delight (and sometimes annoyance) of the elder. Sons always start out on either tea or scoring duties till the day when, either through talent or the more likely non appearance of a player, the son joins in the action and plays his first game. Eventually, the son may take the place of the father in the team and when that day comes the father can contemplate retiring from the team, umpiring and finally taking a watching brief. Not quite the circle of life but certainly the circle of cricket: watch, score, play, umpire and finally, watch again.

Sometimes it can be handy to have a relative umpiring: a certain Melbourne 2nd XI Captain, when umpiring in the 1960s, turned down a leg before wicket appeal. When the bowler enquired as to why, the umpire replied that he couldn't possibly give the batsman out, as the batsman was his nephew and anyway the ball was missing the off stump. Conclusions may be drawn as to which was the greater reason!

These are just some of the fathers, sons and brothers who have played in the same Melbourne XI:
Father G Berrisford; son G Berrisford junior
Father Harry Calvert; son David
Father George Ensor; sons William and Edward
Father Andy Heafield; sons James and Mathew

Father Frank Heafield; son Rodney Heafield
Father Fred Heafield; son Andy
Father Tel Potts; sons Dave and Andy
Father Steve Price; son Farin
Father Derek Tomlinson; son David
Brothers J F and A E Andrews
Brothers C and P Boardman
Brothers Mick and Pete Clough
Brothers William and Edward Ensor
Brothers Kenneth and Gerald Harcombe
Brothers Richard, Stanley and John Hatton
Brothers James and Mathew Heafield
Brothers Phil and Richard Maddocks
Brothers Dave and Andy Potts
Brothers Alex and Matt Slater
Brothers Adrian and Dean Sylvester
Brothers Mark and Paul Winters.

Melbourne 1st XI 1967
Rear L-R: Stan Hatton, Malcom Spare, Derek Hoare, Doug Wilson,
Mrs Turner, Fred Bentley, Frank Ashmore, Mick Clough.
Front L-R, David Baldwin, Roy Grummett, John Turner, Tel Potts,
Lennie Barber. To the right of the group is Ann Pipes (scorer) and in the
background, Peter Whyatt and David Calvert. (44)

THE FUTURE

"For those who recall Bo Derek, she was the perfect 10"

To say that Melbourne is an enthusiastic sporting community is an understatement; it is rather like saying the Pope has a passing interest in religion. Prior to World War 2, for the vast majority of people only the sports of cricket and football existed (many still hold the same view). The town may have had only one cricket team but six football teams competed in separate leagues, many separate organisations having their own teams (Melbourne Young Conservatives, for example) in addition to those representing Melbourne. Currently, the town has clubs for bowls, tennis, badminton, tug of war, football, rugby and cricket. However, for such a sporting community, the town has had very few inhabitants go on to become professional sportsmen or women. Is it something in the Melbourne psyche, as the town has had many 'promising' sportspeople who haven't quite reached the professional rung on the sporting ladder? For the vast majority, life in the town presents a comfortable existence: is it that comfort zone that means the drive to succeed in sport isn't a part of the Melbourne make-up? Another theory takes the view that local sportsmen and women greatly enjoy the success that comes their way as being a part of a Melbourne team, so much so that they are reluctant to come away from that local existence and pursue their sport at higher levels. Of course, professional sport isn't and never should be taken as the yardstick for sporting achievement and many teams have achieved considerable success. The rugby club is thriving and rapidly climbing the league ladder whilst developing their junior teams at an outstanding rate; the Dynamos football team competes in the Midlands Regional Alliance and finished the 2010 season as runners-up. The tennis team finished their season as champions of the Derby area tennis league, division five.

Melbourne Town Cricket Club has ambitious expansion plans and is in the process of raising funds for all-weather nets to be built during the 2011 season. Although currently competing in Divisions Five and Nine South Leagues, the club's forward-thinking plans include the development of the existing coaching structures, a new pavilion and, ultimately, playing at the highest level in the Derbyshire Premier League. Kwik cricket sessions will continue in 2011 and the club has started an under 13s hard ball team which will enter into the local league. The club has entered a team in the indoor cricket league at the Willows Sports Centre and will, once again, be holding winter net practices at the County ground in Derby. Plans are also underway to start girls' and ladies' cricket.

The club believes that junior development is the key to all future developments both on, and off, the playing square.

The club is going through a restructuring process and at the end of 2011 will have sub committees or officers responsible for every aspect of the club. These will include: club development, facility development, selection, ground, junior development, fixtures, commercial, fund raising, sponsorship, membership, communications, publicity and coaching. The club has adopted a development plan for the next four years. All of this will add strength to its off-field activities that exist to complement and develop our on-field activities.

After all, playing cricket is ultimately what we are here to do.

Many of Melbourne's current team's parents and grandparents played for the club as did those of almost all of the committee members. As you would expect from a community based cricket club, plans for the future will be made and carried out with due regard to the club and ground's history and rich local heritage.

However, the club has to be honest and assess the state of its current level of cricket before being able to actually improve it. For those who recall Bo Derek, she was the perfect 10, according to Dudley Moore in the film unsurprisingly called "Ten".

Here are ways for the club to achieve the perfect cricket ten:

1. Long-term thinking will eventually pay off as progress does not happen overnight.

2. Let's cease the politics, self-aggrandisement and vested interests.

3. At any level, a professional approach will lead to success both on and off the pitch.

4. Develop cricketers locally. It doesn't matter if they outgrow the club and seek to better their cricket elsewhere. Take pride in the fact that they started with the club.

5.   Focus on facilities and playing the game properly.

6.   Create junior teams that will ultimately feed the senior teams. We shall give ourselves a chance of success when we identify a 13 year old who eventually blossoms into a fine cricketer and is still playing for us in his mid twenties.

7.   Embrace the shorter forms of cricket but not at the expense of basic cricketing skills.

8.   Infuse the senior squad with up and coming young talent. Junior development doesn't finish with the junior sides. Young players need as much, if not more, looking after when they break into the senior sides.

9.   Selection isn't just about statistics; look at mental and technical cricketing skills.

10. Stop celebrating mediocrity as a source of pride.

We should all remember that sometimes personal triumph will have to take second place to team development and, just occasionally, players will have to take a back seat to greater happenings. On an international level, the great Australian batsman, Sir Donald Bradman, walked out to bat in his last innings at the Oval in 1948 having already announced his retirement. He needed only 4 runs to retire with a test batting average of over 100. England's leg spinner Eric Hollies bowled him first bowl and Bradman walked back to the pavilion to another standing ovation and a test average of 99.99. Hollies commented to the fielder closest to him,

"Best ball I've bowled all season and they're clapping him!"

The future
Melbourne Town's kwik cricket team with club chairman, Tel Potts
and coach Jim Jenkinson. (45)

A – Z DIRECTORY AND BIOGRAPHIES

"When asked what he bowled, instead of the
standard right arm over, he replied, "Fast!""

It was a simple premise; list all players, umpires, the tea ladies and
the great and good who have been associated with the club over the past
150 years. However, this listing is bound to be incomplete as
unfortunately club archives, old scorebooks, web sites and the memories
of cricketers can only provide so much information. For the biography,
again, we have had to rely on what knowledge can be provided and,
regrettably, the only information to hand might be that someone played in
the 1960s.

Adams, G Played in the opening match of the 1871 season against
Kegworth and was out for a duck but went on to play for many more
seasons.

Adcock, Steve Steve was a local player from the late 1970s and early
1980s, a middle order batsman. His greater claim to fame, if possible, is
that he played football for Gresley Rovers at Wembley in the 1991 F A
Vase final.

Alcock, Steve Played in 2006.

Allan, Darren Local young player from the early 1980s.

Allaway, Russell 'Rusty' is the 1st XI wicketkeeper and a regular run
getter. Recently moved to Northampton but still travels to play.

Anderson, Tom Classy batsman who now plays for Swarkestone but
played for Melbourne early in his career. Scored 98 against Littleover
Centurions in 1998.

Andrews, A E A member of the 1912 Derby and District League
Championship team. One of the Andrews family who were all
exceptionally fine cricketers. Captain of the 1st XI in 1928. He took 6
wickets for 17 runs playing against Bemrose and Sons in June 1890.

Andrews, Arthur Played for the club on August 18th 1875 against a
Derby XI and also appeared in the 1895 batting averages. It is unclear
whether he is related to the other Andrews.

Andrews, E   A member of the 1912 Derby and District League Championship team and another member of the Andrews cricketing family.

Andrews, Hugh   Vice Chairman of the club in the 1970s and a member of the Andrews family who were all exceptionally fine cricketers. The last of the great Andrews dynasty to be associated with the club. Hughie was also an accomplished photographer who captured much of Melbourne life on film.

Andrews, J F   Batsman who played in the winning 1912 Derby and District League Championship decider between the MTCC and Spondon, making 102 runs out of a total of 157. A member of the Andrews family who were all exceptionally fine cricketers. Club Secretary for 30 years from 1898 to 1928.

Archer, S   Won the best bowling award in 1896 and also took 4 wickets playing against Woodville in the same year. He must have been an excellent all-rounder as he was second in the 1895 batting averages.

Argyle, A   2nd XI Vice Captain in 1928.

Armitage, R   Player from the 1960s.

Ashmore, Frank   Player from the 1950s and umpire in the 1960s.

Astle, J   Played against Ashby on September 10th 1862 and scored 6 runs.

Astle, W   Played against Ashby on September 10th 1862 and scored 7 runs.

Audlinword, M   Played against Ashby on July 20th 1870 and scored 25 runs.

Bacon, A   Played in the late 1990s; average of 21 and a high score of 23 in the 1996 season.

Bacon, S   Played in the late 1990s; average of 21.07 and a high score of 64 in the 1997 season.

Bailey, Mark   Captain of the 1st XI in 1990; a very good all-round cricketer. Batting average of 43.9 and high score of 103 not out in the 1995 season. Played in the 1st XI that gained successive promotions .in the early 2000s.

Baldwin, David   David played for the club in the early 1960s.

Barber, Lennie   See Ch 8 - The Lothian Trophy and Melbourne Legends.

Bareham, Mick   Club scorer for many years whose efforts were always well appreciated. Would regularly announce his retirement at the club dinner at the end of each season only to reappear the next, full of enthusiasm.

Barker, John   'Fred' was an all-rounder, a good fielder and an opening bowler who you could rely on for line and length. Still lives locally. Took 22 wickets in the 1992 season for the 2nd XI at an average of 12.5.

Barrett, William   Player of the 1930s who was Headmaster of the Board School in High Street and Chairman of the club for many years. Captain of the 2nd XI in 1928 and the 1st XI in 1933.

Barrington, G   Played against Alvaston on September 15th 1869 and was run out for 4 runs.

Barson, G   A player from the very early days of the club who appeared in the 1860s.

Bavister, Andy   Bavi is a player of the current era who's always good company both on and off the pitch.

Baxter, David   Played for the 1st XI in the 1970s; a very good and stylish batsman.

Baxter, R   Groundsman in 1904.

Melbourne 1st XI 1964
Rear L-R: Lennie Barber, Roy Grummett, Clive Burton, Malcom Spare,
Mick Clough, Charles (Bud) Toon, Frank Ashmore.
Front L-R: Richard Hatton, John Turner, Fred Bentley,
Harold Hodgkinson, Dennis Dunnicliffe. (46)

Beardsley, Ernie Player from the 1950s and committee member; also the local printer and leader of a popular dance band of the time, the Ernie Beardsley Trio.

Beardsley, J Played in the opening match of the 1871 season against Kegworth and was not out for 4 runs.

Beardsley, Lol Player from the mid 1950s who scored 35 against Crewton Sports on July 2nd 1955.

Beardsley, Paul Bins was a good all-round sportsman, perhaps better known as a local footballer. Played in the 1970s.

Bell, Clarence Bowled the opening ceremonial ball when the ground and pavilion was reopened on May 12th 1951 after closing down for World War 2.

Bentley, Brenda Brenda (Parnham) was the wife of Fred Bentley and a tea lady in the 1960s.

Bentley, Frederick Fred was Captain of the 1st XI from 1958 to 1965 when the club arguably had its golden period, reaching the final of the Butterley Cup in 1965. Took 5 wickets for 39 runs against Castle Donington on July 23rd 1955. One of the club's longest serving captains.

Bentley, Jean Jean was the wife of Sergeant Bentley, mother of Fred and a tea lady in the 1960s.

Bentley, Sergeant Sergeant Bentley umpired in the 1950s and 60s and was the father of Fred.

Berrisford, junior, G A player from the very early days of the club who appeared in the 1860s playing alongside his father.

Berrisford, senior, G A player from the very early days of the club who appeared in the 1860s playing alongside his son.

Bhatti, K Played in the mid 1980s.

Bhuman, Chanda Played in 2009 in the Loughborough League.

Bishop, A Player from the 1960s.

Blackburn, H Player of the 1930s who succeeded AC Goodband as headteacher of the National School in Penn Lane. A Yorkshireman and, as you would expect, a very enthusiastic cricketer. Captain of the 2nd XI in 1932.

Blinco, Daniel Young local player from the mid 1980s who went on to join the Army and tragically lost his life in 1993 whilst serving with the Grenadier Guards in Northern Ireland when only 22 years of age. His former comrades still meet every year on Remembrance Sunday in Melbourne.

Blood, J W   A member of the 1912 Derby and District League Championship team.

Blood, Jack   Played in the team that reopened the cricket facilities on May 12th 1951 after the club and ground had closed down during the World War 2.

Blood, John   Brother of Quentin who played for the club in the middle 1970s. A very enthusiastic cricketer. When asked by one umpire what he bowled when coming on at Ticknall, instead of the standard "right arm over", he replied "Fast!".

Blood, Quentin   Brother of John; a very keen medium fast-bowler.

Blood, W   A batting average of 18 in the 1895 season and also played against Kegworth in 1900.

Bloor, S   Umpire in 1939.

What else is there to do in winter? Melbourne indoor team, early 1970s
Rear L-R: John Hallifield, Steve Tivey, George Harris
Front L-R: Alan Bradley, Stuart Pegg, Anthony Crowson. (47)

Blount, M Local player from the mid 1980s.

Boardman, Christopher Chris played in the mid 1950s. Brother of Peter and the son of Dr Hedley Boardman. He scored 73 not out against SBL Cricket Club on August 20th 1955.

Boardman, Dr Hedley Dr Boardman was a leading member of the committee that called a public meeting in 1950 to reinstate the club and ground after World War 2. He was the chairman for many years afterwards and a great supporter of local cricket.

Boardman, Peter Pete played in the mid 1950s. Brother of Chris and son of Dr Hedley Boardman.

Bolton, Chris Played in 2007 and 2008.

Borrington, Anthony See Ch 11 - Melbourne Cricketers Who Played First Class Cricket.

Bowes, Nick Current club umpire who played league cricket prior to taking up the white coat.

Boyd, Dave Good all-rounder from the current era of players.

Boyes, Jonny Played in 2009 in the Loughborough League.

Bradley, Adrian Younger brother of Alan. One of the club's youngest players who, like many before him, started out as the club scorer. A boy with great sporting promise, he died whilst still a youngster and is still remembered by many at the club with great affection.

Bradley, Alan The Brad was a true all-rounder, wicketkeeper and local postman. He captained the Sunday and 2nd XI teams to some success with both teams enjoying his captaincy and the social side of cricket whilst he was at the helm. Played in the 2010 Legends game where he was injured playing forward and had to be carried off the pitch. Topped the bowling averages for the 2nd XI in 1992. Still watches on Saturdays after a stint at the adjacent allotments.

Briers, Gary Played in the mid 1990s; took 23 wickets in the 1996 season for the 2nd XI.

Briggs, G Played against Coleorton in 1893 and scored 11 runs.

Briggs, W Captain of the club in 1892.

Brown, J Played against Long Whatton on September 2nd 1863 and scored a duck but went on to play for many more seasons.

Brunton, G Played in the team that reopened the cricket facilities on May 12th 1951 after the club and ground had closed down during the World War 2.

Bull, Martin Martin was one of the many young players from Bemrose School, brought to the club in the 1960s by Harry Calvert. He went on to play for Elvaston where he met with a tragic and untimely death. During a first team match in 1983 he was struck on the chest by a ball that slipped from the bowlers hands in the wet conditions. He collapsed and never regained consciousness despite attempts at revival. In his memory, cherry trees were planted at Elvaston that flower every April.

Burton, Clive   Clive played in the 1960s; he was a very good all-round cricketer and played a high standard of football for Belper Town.

Burton, Helen   Helen is the fianceé of James Smith; 2nd XI scorer and provider of very good cricket teas.

Buxton, Alan   'Bucko' is also the Joint Manager of the Melbourne Dynamos football team and one of the many footballers to have been drafted in to play cricket for MTCC.

Byers, Mark   Played in 2009 in the Loughborough League.

Calow, F   Played against Ashby on September 10th 1862. He scored four runs and took one catch.

Calvert, David   Son of Harry and nicknamed 'Killer' for his work in the slips. The title of this book comes from one spectator who, having seen him take a catch, exclaimed "He dove 'n' ketched it!" A cricketer of great determination and passion. Now a Vice President of the Club who worked for the Midland Bank prior to retirement. Having lived away from the area for many years, he has moved back and has a prominent role in many local organisations, including the Probus Club, the Scouts and the Allotment Society. David played in the 1950s and 1960s.

Calvert, Harry   Harry is fondly remembered by generations of cricketers and particularly those who attended Bemrose Grammar School in Derby where he was a maths teacher, head of the Philatelic Society and the organiser of the under 13s cricket team. He would reward good shots, bowling and fielding by passing round the Spangles, Olde English flavour, of course. He would exhort the youngsters in the Melbourne teams to get down whilst fielding the ball but would cheerfully ignore his own instructions when the cherry came his way. He captained the 2nd XI in the 1970s.

Carroll, T   Played in the 1993 season.

Carter, Nick   Big Nick is an import from Alvaston who went on to become a great favourite with fellow players. Still living locally and running Melbourne Carpets, whilst balancing his work in between rounds of golf with daughter, Evie, who plays for the county. Played in the 2010 Legends match and in the 1st XI that gained successive promotions in the early 2000s.

Chambers, R E J   See Ch 11 - Melbourne Cricketers Who Played First Class Cricket.

Chapman, Dave Played in 2009 in the Loughborough League.

Clarke, Daniel Played in 2008.

Clarke, Sam Played in 2006.

Clayton, Cliff   Cliff played in the 1950s including the Melbourne and District XI against a Derbyshire XI in the testimonial match for Cliff Gladwin on Sunday July 5th 1953. He captained the 2nd XI in 1954 and in that season, playing for the Sunday XI, made a century against Breedon, who at that time were one of the top teams in the area.

Clough, Mick   Brother of Pete and a fine batsman who played in the 1960s.

Clough, Pete See Ch 8 - The Lothian Trophy and Living Legends.

Coath, Dennis   Was the Sports Editor for Central News. In his time there he interviewed top sports personalities including Muhammed Ali, Bjorn Borg, Stanley Mathews and Brian Clough. Played for the club in the 1990s and was an excellent all-round cricketer. He is also an accomplished writer and wrote 'Deep Cover' with Ian Botham. Averaged 21.12 for the 2nd XI in the 1998 season with a high score of 26 and took 17 wickets in the same season.

Cockeram, Mr   Played against Alvaston on September 15th 1869 and scored 5 runs.

Collyer, A Captain of the 2nd XI in 1910.

Collyer, Denys Denys played in the 1950s and was a very good batsman. A market gardener all his working life; his son Nigel is the chairman of the Melbourne Parish Council.

Collyer, T Played against Ashby on September 10th 1862 and scored 3 not out.

Cook, F Took 47 wickets in the 1892 season at an average of 6.22.

Cook, F W   Played against Ashby on September 10th 1862 and scored 5 runs. He played against them eight years later in 1870 and was run out for the same total. Played in the 1895 season, bowled 102 overs and took 15 wickets. Vice Captain of the club in 1892.

Cook, J A player from the very early days of the club who appeared in the 1860s and played for many years.

Cowlishaw, M Local player from the early 1980s.

Coxon, J Played against Ashby on September 10th 1862 and scored 4 runs.

Cripps, James 'Crippys' is the landlord of the Alma Inn in Melbourne. Originally from Chellaston, he will no doubt be fully accepted into Melbourne life in another 25 years. Server of a fine pint of Marston's Pedigree. Plays for the 2nd XI, having previously played for Swarkestone.

Cripps, Mr A wicketkeeper and proprietor of the Gayborder Nurseries in Kings Newton, who played in the 1930s.

Croake, Garry Played in 2007.

Croft, A An all-rounder who played in the late 1980s and early 90s.

Croft, J B Local player from the mid 1980s.

Croft, M Local player from the mid 1980s to early 1990s. Highest score of 23 in the 1990 season.

Crossley, Richard A good all-rounder who played and captained the 2nd XI in the 1960s and 1970s. Played and captained the successful Dynamos football team of that era.

Crowson, Anthony Ant was a Breedon born left-handed batsman of considerable talent and volcanic temperament who ended his playing days at neighbouring Swarkestone. Son, Isaac, captains their 3rd XI.

Daffern, John Player from the 1960s and son-in-law of Harry Calvert.

Dallman, H Played against Worthington and company on August 3rd 1870 and was 0 not out.

Dando, John Dando played in the 1970s through to the 1990s and was a very good bowler who in one glorious season took 100 wickets for the club. He would think nothing of bowling unchanged from one end and was also a very underrated batsman. Club Secretary for a while, he captained both the 1st and 2nd XI teams.

Dickman, Alf Captain of the 1st XI in 1952 who played for the Melbourne and District XI against a Derbyshire XI in the A E Rhodes testimonial match. A keen supporter of the British Legion in Melbourne: the bar there is called 'Alf's Bar'.

Dickman, Mark Dicko has just started playing indoor cricket for the club at a late age and is finally following in the footsteps of his father and grandfather.

Dickman, William Bill played from the mid 1950s and into the 1960s. The son of Alf and father of Mark.

Dochery, Neil Played in 2005.

Dolman, Adam A good all-rounder who won the Sunday bowling trophy in 2001. Plays football for the Melbourne Dynamos.

Donald, L Player from the mid 1990s, with a high score of 22 for the 2nd XI in 1998.

Dore, B Player from the early 1990s. Top score of 58 in the 1995 season for the 2nd XI.

Draper, Harold Harold was the scorer when a Melbourne and District XI played against Cliff Gladwin's XI in Cliff's testimonial match on July 5th 1953. He also umpired for the club.

Draper, J K Played in the team that reopened the cricket facilities on May 12th 1951 after the club and ground had closed down during World War 2 and was secretary that year.

Dunnicliff, Eric Played in the team that reopened the cricket facilities on May 12th 1951 after the club and ground had closed down during World War 2. He also played in the Cliff Gladwin testimonial match in 1953. The Dunnicliff family owned the shoe factory in Derby Road.

Dunnicliffe, Frank Captained the team that reopened the cricket facilities on May 12th 1951 after the club and ground had closed down during World War 2. Also Captain of the 2nd XI in 1936.

Dunnicliffe, Dennis See Ch 8 - The Lothian Trophy and Living Legends.

Dunnicliffe, G Played against Kegworth in 1900 and scored 12 runs.

Earl, George Burrill See Ch 11 - Melbourne Cricketers Who Played First Class Cricket.

Earp, A Player from the 1960s.

Earp, A Player from the late 1970s and 1980s who played against Derby Congs in 1979 when Melbourne were all out for 6.

Elliott, P Player from the mid 1950s.

English, Ivan Player from the mid 1990s who took 27 wickets for the 2nd XI in 1996.

Ensor, Edward Son of George Ensor and brother of William. Played in the 1950s.

Ensor, George Player in the 1930s; umpire in the 1967 Butterley Cup Final and in the game when the club and ground was reopened on May 12th 1951 after closing down for World War 2. Father of William and Edward. Umpired in the testimonial matches held for Cliff Gladwin and A E Rhodes.

Ensor, W A player from the very early days of the club who appeared in the 1870s and was also recorded as playing against Kegworth in 1900. Groundsman in 1921.

Ensor, William Son of George Ensor and brother of Edward. Played in the 1950s.

Faiz, R Played in the mid 1980s and scored 44 against Mickleover on September 1st 1984.

Farmer, Bas   Bas would often bat with no protection on his hands, preferring to use the bat to great effect instead, regularly launching sixes in to what was then Hatton's Yard. Moved to Melbourne after playing for Breedon CC. At the time Breedon were THE big club in the area, regularly attracting a thousand spectators to their Sunday games. Played in the 1965 Butterley Cup Final and can be ranked as one of the club's best all-rounders.

Fazal, Tariq   All-rounder who played in the early 90s batting average of 22.5 and took 10 wickets in the 1990 season.

Fiddler, Ian   All-rounder who has played since 2005.

Fisher, T   Player from the mid 1990s high score of 50 for the 2nd XI in 1998.

Fletcher, Paul   Paul is a Derbyshire lad who has always enjoyed his sport. He played football, rugby and cricket to County schoolboy level and enjoyed some great times playing for Darley Dale at cricket. He moved to Melbourne, with wife Liz, in 1996. He coaches cricket at under eleven level, where son William is a budding all-rounder.

Fletcher, W   Played in the late 1980s and early 1990s.

Floyd, S   Local player from the late 1970s and early 1980s. Played in the match against Derby Congs when Melbourne were 6 all out.

Foddy, A   Captain of the 2nd XI in 1933.

Footitt, Daniel   Played in 2009 in the Loughborough League.

Foster, Robert   Played in 2005.

Gadsby, Aubrey   Big hitting, left-handed, Aubrey was one of several young lads who came over from Breedon along with Richard North and Tony Wileman. Played in the late 1960s.

Garnett, Tim   Played in 2005.

Garratt, Bernard   A great character and player from the 1960s.

Gee, Tony   Played in the late 1960s and early 1970s. A promising bowler and good all-round cricketer with a terrific throw.

Gibson, Rich   Played in 2009 in the Loughborough League.

Gillam, Mr   Played against Alvaston on September 15th 1869 and scored 5 runs.

Goodband, A C   Player of the 1930s and Headmaster of the National School in Penn Lane. Captained the 1st XI in 1921; an athletic wicketkeeper.

Goodwin, C   Player from the mid 1990s with a high score of 2 not out in 1995.

Grant, Ken   Kenny G played for Elvaston prior to Melbourne. The current groundsman and the 2nd XI's very stylish opening batsman, wicketkeeper and Captain. Played in the Harry Lund Cup Final in 2010 and came agonisingly close to scoring 1,000 runs in the same season.

Gray, Noel   Son of Sid who, whilst watching his dad play, became the team scorer in the late 1950s.

Gray, Robert   Player from the 1950s who played for the Melbourne and District XI against a Derbyshire XI in the A E Rhodes testimonial on July 6th 1952.

Gray, Sid   Sid played in the team that reopened the cricket facilities on May 12th 1951 after the club and ground had closed down during World War 2. He was born in Melbourne in 1914. He was a good all-rounder who also played football for Melbourne Town. Sid worked on the land locally for Maurice Collyer.

Griffiths, Sylvia   One of the tea ladies of the 1960s. Still living in Melbourne and married to Stuart Tomlinson.

Grummett, Lisa and Sarah   Daughters of Roy, who did the teas when he was skipper of the 1st XI. Both daughters still live in Melbourne.

Grummett, Roy   See Ch 8 - The Lothian Trophy and Living Legends.

Guildford, Kevin   Local young player from the early 1980s. Very good footballer for the Melbourne Dynamos Sunday team.

Gunn, Luke   Played in 2009 in the Loughborough League.

Hallifield, John   Big John has played 45 consecutive seasons for the club, starting in 1966. His record is unlikely to be matched as he is still playing and hopes to carry on till he reaches the milestone of 50 consecutive seasons in 2015. Fast-bowler and French teacher, now retired. With his height, his bowling was always very effective and even now has a sting to it. Captain of the 2nd XI in 1990. Scored 66 against Diseworth on September 23rd 1978. Took 7 wickets for 13 runs against Copsey Croft on July 7th 1979.

Hallifield, Victor   Christened Victor but universally known as Vinny; promising young 2nd XI batsman who was a convert from football, he still plays for the Melbourne Dynamos. From a Ticknall farming family, but nobody holds that against him. Played in the Harry Lund Cup Final in 2010. Captains the indoor team. On August 7th 2007 against Castle Donington he was a part of a 100 run partnership with Mike Starkie. Mike scored 85 not out; Vinny scored 0; extras 15!

Harcombe, Gerald   Player from the 1930s and son of the local vicar brother of Kenneth.

Harcombe, Kenneth   Player from the 1930s and son of the local vicar; brother of Gerald.

Harper, G   Played against Worthington and company on August 3rd 1870 and scored 3 not out.

Harris, George   One of the nicest people you could ever come across; would apologise for anything and everything, even if you ran him out. Very unassuming and a much better player than he gave himself credit for. A good all-rounder. Scored 51 against Crusaders on April 22nd 1979 and 96 against Kirk Langley on August 4th 1979.

Harris, R   2nd XI umpire in 1928.

Harrison, Frazer   Startlingly fast bowler of repute whose father and grandfather both played for Ticknall CC. In the 2000 season, took 49 wickets at an average of 12.81 and in 1999 took 56 wickets. Finished playing too early so don't rule out a comeback.

Harrison, John   A classy batsman of some distinction who is now our district and county councillor. Chairman of the club in 2001 and now chairman of the Melbourne Sporting Partnership, which is hoping to develop the ground facilities in the very near future.

Harvey, Maurice   Maurice was a popular player from the 1950s and 60s who played a very good standard of cricket. Prior to playing for Melbourne he played for Breedon who, at that time, were one of the top clubs of the area.

Hasard, J   Played against Ashby on September 10th in 1862 and had the 'distinction' of being caught by the Marquis of Hastings for 1 run.

Hassan, R   Played in the early 1990s; high score of 40 in the 1995 season for the 2nd XI.

Hatton, Albert James   Albert was the captain of the 2nd XI in 1908 and was also the 1st XI scorer when the club won the 1907 championship.

Hatton, Barbara   Barbara was the wife of Stan and a tea lady in the 1960s.

Hatton, John Reginald   John played in the team that reopened the cricket facilities on May 12th 1951 after the club and ground had closed down during World War 2. He served as the secretary of the club in the 1950s and was the eldest of the six Hatton brothers who included Richard and Stan. He started work as a delivery boy for the Melbourne Co-op at the age of 14 and went on to work for them all of his life. He was a member of the Melbourne Round Table and then the 40s club.

Hatton, Richard Kenneth   Wicketkeeper and groundsman for many years, a resolute servant to the club and cricket. Played in the 1965 Butterley Cup Final and was in the team that reopened the ground in 1951. He was the chairman of the club in the 1970s and also captained the 2nd XI during that period.

Hatton, Stanley Alan Stan was a steady left arm slow bowler who toiled away with guile and flight for many years from the Hatton's Yard end. His daughter played cricket for England Women's Indoor team. He first played in 1954 and carried on playing well into the 1990s. After playing, Stan went on to umpire for the 1st XI. He completed 50 years of service to the club in 2004.

Hatton, William William played in the opening match of the 1871 season against Kegworth and scored 1 run.

Hawksworth, J Player from the mid 1950s.

Haynes, D Player from the 1960s.

Hazledine, R All-rounder from the mid 1980s.

1965 Butterley Cup Finalists
Rear L-R: Richard Hatton, Fred Bentley, Derek Hoare, Bas Farmer,
Stan Hatton, Dennis Dunnicliffe, George Ensor.
Front L-R: Alan Staniforth, Roy Grummett, Tel Potts, John Turner, Lennie
Barber, Pete Whyatt. (48)

Heafield, Andrew Andy is the son of Fred and first played when he was 12 years old in 1967. In 1978 went to play for Ticknall and in 1983 moved to London for 25 years where he played cricket for the Blacksmiths Arms

XI. He returned to resume playing for Melbourne in 2009. That is probably the longest spell between games for any member of the club. Author of this book.

Heafield, Charles Frederick   See Ch 8 - The Lothian Trophy and Living Legends.

Heafield, Frank   See Ch 8 - The Lothian Trophy and Living Legends.

Heafield, James   Jimbo is the grandson of Fred and son of Andy. Bowler and batsman who is an excellent golfer. A high score of 35 against Edwalton in 2010; he also keeps wicket.

Heafield, Mathew   Matt is the grandson of Fred and son of Andy. Bowler and batsman who played for the club when 13 years old. He also played in the Harry Lund Cup Final in 2010 and was a County triallist in the same year. Scored 79 not out against Ticknall in 2010.

Heafield, Rodney   Rod was a player of the 1960s and the son of Frank, who worked at the local Midland Bank in Melbourne before retirement. Still a regular spectator at matches and a daily customer, with his father, at the Welcome Cafe in Melbourne.

Heath, Jonathan   2nd XI opening bat of the 1980s and grandson of Richard.

Heath, Keiran   2nd XI player from 2006.

Heath, Richard   Current Club President and local historian. What he doesn't know about Melbourne isn't worth knowing and he serves the community on many local committees, including the Royal British Legion.

Hemsley, J   A player from the very early days of the club who played in the 1860s.

Hibbert, F   Played against Long Whatton on September 2nd 1863 and scored 5 runs.

Hicklin, Alan   The son of Ike. Alan scored for Melbourne and played one game for the Melbourne 2nd XI in the 1960s under the captaincy of Harold Hodgkinson. Alan lives in Station Road, Melbourne.

Hicklin, Ike   Ike was a very good all-round sportsman who originally played for Breedon during the late 1950s and early 1960s and then came to play for Melbourne. He captained the 2nd XI before going on to play for the 1st XI. He played football for Stanton Villa and also boxed professionally at welterweight.

Hicklin, Rod   Big Rod is a larger than life all-rounder from the 1970s who has just returned to the village; always good company.

Hickling, J   Played 15 matches in the 1895 season.

No diesel fuelled roller in those days c1962
L-R: Clive Burton, Lennie Barber, Roy Grummett,
Harold Hodgkinson, John Turner, Mick Clough. (49)

Hills, Richard Played from 2005 to 2007.

Hoare, Derek Foremark Hall and Repton school teacher and all-rounder who played in the 1965 Butterley Cup Final. He also recruited many players from the school to play for the club.

Hodgkinson, Harold First played for the club in the 1930s and was still playing when the club resumed play after World War 2. Went on to be Secretary from 1958 to 1972 and captained the 2nd team from 1957 to 1963.

Holder, Frank Played in 2009 in the Loughborough League and for the 2nd XI.

Holdgate, Matt Played in 2008.

Hollingsworth, F 2nd XI scorer in 1929.

Holmes, H Played against Alvaston on September 15th 1869 and scored 34 runs. He is recorded as being thrown out, possibly referring to a direct hit on the stumps when attempting a run.

Hood, W Played against Ashby on July 20th 1870, scored 11 runs and took 5 wickets.

Horsley, James Jim is the only MTCC player to have gone on to play county cricket. See Ch 10 - MTCC Legend and County cricketer.

Horsley, John   Played against Draycott on May 31st 1893, scoring 26 runs. The father of Jim Horsley. He also took 27 wickets in the 1893 season.

Elliott H.   Carter. W.   Bestwick. W.   Horsley J.   Hutchinson J.(I).   Bowden J.
(Morton. A.   W. W. Hill-Wood.   G.R.Jackson.   Cadman. S.   Storer. H.

Jim Horsley, early in his Derbyshire career
Rear L-R: H Elliott, W Carter, W Bestwick,
Jim Horsley, J I Hutchinson, J Bowden.
Front L-R: A Morton, W W Hill-Wood, G R Jackson, S Cadman, H Storer. (50)

Houghton, James   'Jim' was a player from the 1950s who played in the testimonial match for A E Rhodes on July 6th 1952 and for the Melbourne and District XI against a Derbyshire XI in the testimonial match for Cliff Gladwin on Sunday July 5th 1953. He took 7 wickets for 12 runs against Swarkestone on June 25th 1955. Jim was a very fine fast bowler.

Houghton, W   A player from the very early days of the club who appeared in the 1860s.

Hughes-Hallet, Norton Montresor See Ch 11 - Melbourne Players Who Played First Class Cricket.

Hunt, F B Captain of the 1st XI in 1939 and a very skilful slow bowler.

Hurst, Clinton A promising young player who has just joined the club. Hopefully, he has a long cricket career ahead of him.

Hutchinson, F Umpire in 1937.

Illsley, E J A member of the 1912 Derby and District League Championship team. A batting average of 12.25 in the 1895 season.

Jackson, Gerald Player from the 1960s who still lives locally and can be seen at Melbourne football matches and the British Legion.

Jackson, R Player from the 1960s.

Jackson, Tom Played in the 1970s. What he lacked in ability he more than made up for in enthusiasm. Last heard of working in Sudan. A great sense of humour.

Jackson, Vic Player from the 1950s who played for the Melbourne and District XI against a Derbyshire XI in the A E Rhodes testimonial match on July 6th 1952. A highly rated fast-bowler who opened the attack with Charles 'Bud' Toon.

James, P Player from the mid 1950s who took 4 wickets for 8 runs against Draycott on August 13th 1955.

Jenkinson, Jim Jim was originally from Lincolnshire and moved to Melbourne in 2005. He spent many summers watching his dad play cricket and naturally grew up with a bat in his hand. He played school and club cricket but was a better rugby player. He is our current kwik cricket coach and is married to Claire who is a P E teacher. It's no surprise that sons, Sam and Joe, enjoy their sport.

Jerome, L Played against Long Whatton on September 2nd 1863 and scored 2 runs.

Jessani, Sal Classy bowler and batsman who currently plays for the 1st XI.

Jesson, Gary A good cricketer who always gives everything both on and off the pitch. Gary is organising the club tour in 2014 to Melbourne, Australia. G'day!

Jones, N Local player from the mid 1980s.

Keeling, J Played against Ashby on July 20th 1870 and scored 2 runs.

Keith-Reid, J K Played in the team that reopened the cricket facilities on May 12th 1951 after the club and ground had closed down during World War 2 and went on to become Secretary in the late 50s.

Kendal, V A fast-bowler from the 1930s with a windmill action and long run up.

Khan, Urfan Played in the 1992 season with a batting average of 14 and taking 10 wickets.

Kincey, F A player from the very early days of the club who appeared in the 1870s.

Kirk, W Played against Ashby on July 20th 1870 and was thrown out for 1 run.

Kirkman, Mrs One of the tea ladies of the 1960s.

Kirkman, R Player from the 1960s.

Knipe, J H A member of the 1912 Derby and District League Championship team.

Lacey, Joe A product of the Ticknall youth system who brings his stylish batting to the MTCC 2nd XI. Ticknall's loss has been our gain. Coach of the newly formed under 13s team.

Lacey, Marg Mother of Joe and Richard who always helps with the club's fund raising activities.

Lacey, Richard Local player from the mid 1980s and brother of Joe.

Lakin, Ray Captain of the 2nd XI in 1976 who continued to lead the side for many seasons. A good bowler, renowned for occasionally wearing a black belt with his white cricket flannels.

Lancaster, Chris Good all-rounder who has captained our Sunday XI. Bats and bowls with a classic style and is one of the club's main cheerleaders on the field. A good golfer who married Caroline in 2010.

Lane , C Captain of the 2nd XI in 1936.

Laurie, Paul Good club cricketer from the 1990s who now lives in Dubai. Topped the 2nd XI batting averages in 2000 with a high score of 158 not out against Cromford. He must have liked their bowling as he scored 102 against the same opponents in the same season.

Laxton, R Local player from the early 1980s.

Leech, Graham Left-handed bowler who played for the club whilst at school. Still bowling locally, but of the flat green variety at Kings Newton.

Long, James Played in 2007.

Lovell, Neil A good bat and wicketkeeper from the 1980s who played in the Legends match in 2010. Scored 73 against Ticknall on June 2nd 1984.

Maddocks, Phil Brother of Richard. Rugby playing cricketer who bats well for the 1st XI and has many years to play in front of him. First played in 1995. Played in the 1st XI that gained successive promotions in the early 2000s.

Maddocks, Richard Brother of Phil who also plays rugby. A good all-round sportsman.

Manning, Olly A good cricketer and clubman; played for the 2nd XI in the early 2000s. High score of 101 and an average of 32.07 in 2003.

Manukondo, Chandra Played in 2008.

Marshall, Daniel Dan is the son of Robert and a left arm medium pacer who we hope will be playing for the club for years to come. Coach of the under 13s cricket team.

Marshall, Robert 'Marsh' played for the 2nd XI for many seasons. A very thoughtful cricketer and great company on those rainy cricket days when far too much time is spent in the pavilion. A good off spinner and much underrated batsman. Captain of the 2nd XI in 1975.

Marshall, S Player from the 1960s.

Mason, W 1st XI umpire in 1928.

Massey, George George played for the club in the 1960s.

Matthews, R Played against Aston on Trent in August 1900.

Mayers, John Current player and sponsor who is a good all-rounder. In the 1991 season he had a batting average of 20 with a high score of 70 not out for the 2nd XI.

Meakin, Mick All-rounder who formerly played for Mickleover. Capable of getting runs and wickets with his steady medium swing bowling. Regularly features in the League's top bowlers and batsmen. Now playing for Elvaston after leaving the club in 2010.

Mee, A Player from the mid 1950s.

Middleton, L Played against Long Whatton on September 2nd 1863 scoring 8 runs and taking 2 wickets.

Moore, Gary Played for the 1st XI in 1999 and won the fielding trophy that year.

Mosey, J Player from the 1960s.

Moulton, T Player from the mid 1990s; high score of 21 in 1995.

Neale, H Played against Ashby on September 19th 1862; scored 9 runs and took 1 wicket.

Newberry, M A Player from the 1950s who played for the Melbourne and District XI against a Derbyshire XI in the testimonial match for Cliff Gladwin on Sunday July 5th 1953.

Newbold, H Played in the 1892 season and had a batting average of 9.3; good enough to put him 4th overall in the club.

Newbold, W A Captain of the 1st XI in 1904. Topped the batting and bowling averages in 1895.

Newton, Ben 'Newts' is a fast-bowler currently playing for the 1st XI. On his day, very capable of running through the opposition. He is also a hard hitting lower order batsman.

North, Richard A good all-rounder who came over from Breedon with Tony Wileman & Aubrey Gadsby to play for the 2nd XI in the late 1960s.

Ogden, Eric Local player from the mid 1980s who also played for Derby Banks.

Parry, P Player from the 1960s.

Parry, Terence Fast-bowler and one of many Bemrose schoolboys brought to the club by Harry Calvert in the early 1970s. A part of the Derby Parry footballing family that included Jack and Tony.

Payne, E Player from the 1960s.

Payne, T Player from the mid 1950s who took 4 wickets for 16 runs against Swarkestone on August 8th 1955.

Pearce, Keith Good clubman and cricketing character from the 1970s and 1980s. Never gave anything less than 100% for the club.

Pedley, D Played in the late 1990s; batting average of 26.16 with a high score of 44 in the 1997 season for the 1st XI. High score of 86 not out for the 2nd XI in 1995.

Pegg, I Player from the mid 1990s.

Pegg, M Player from the mid 1990s. In 1998, took 54 wickets for the 2nd XI and 51 in the 1999 season.

Pegg, Stuart Derby Boys footballer who played for the club whilst still at school. Now residing in Burton on Trent but played in the 2010 Legends game. A very good all-round player. Scored 47 against B R Erectors on August 25th 1984.

Pegg , K Player from the 1960s.

Perambulator, Mr Amazingly, he appears as playing for the club on October 4th 1871 scoring 47 runs. With his surname and obvious batting ability he may have been playing under an assumed name?

Perry, James Captain of the 2nd XI in 1995. Took 16 wickets and averaged 15 runs that season.

Philbrick, J Player from the 1960s.

Pincket, F Played against Ashby on September 10th 1862 and was out for a duck. Went on to play for many more years.

Pipes, Anne Anne helped Mrs Turner with the teas in the 1960s.

Pipes, Daniel A good cricketer and fielder who won the 1st XI fielding trophy in 2008.

Plackett, F Played against Long Whatton on September 2nd 1863 and scored a duck but took 5 wickets.

Potts, Andy Son of Tel Potts and a genuine all-rounder who played for the club as a youngster and has gone on to be a regular opening batsman and bowler for the 1st XI. Scored 121 for the 1st XI against Lullington on July 13th 2008. Played in the 1st XI that gained successive promotions in the early 2000s.

Potts, Dave Son of Tel Potts and an off spinner who played in the Harry Lund Cup Final in 2010, making them the only father and son in the club's history to play in both finals that Melbourne has reached. A regular taker of wickets with an almost unique delivery stride. Took 55 wickets for the 2nd XI in 1995 at an average of 15.90.

Potts, Gail Wife of Dave and supplier of high class teas.

Potts, Harry Son of Dave Potts and grandson of Tel. Played in the 2010 Legends game when 8 years old trapping Tel leg before (the video replay was inconclusive) and bowling father Dave.

Potts, John Groundsman in the 1950s and the father of Tel. Surprisingly, he never played.

Potts, Sue Wife of Tel and the current club treasurer who also plays a big part in the organisation of the Kwik cricket teams.

Potts, Terence Tel is the current club Chairman who played in the 1965 Butterley Cup as a raw 16 year old. First played for the club as a 12 year old. A bludgeoning left-handed batsman, wicketkeeper, athletic fielder and pacey bowler, who always gave his best for the club on the field and now does the same off it. Captained both 1st and 2nd XI teams with unbridled enthusiasm.

Poynton, C Player from the 1960s.

Pratt, J Played in the late 1980s and early 1990s; batting average of 8.17 with a high score of 23 in 1990.

Preston, Andy Local player from the early 1980s.

Preston, Mark Played in the early 1990s; batting average of 21.25 in 1991 and took 3 wickets. Highest score of 57 in 1992.

Price, D Local player from the mid 1980s.

Price, Farin Fazzer is the son of Steve Price. He is a good medium pace bowler and steady bat who has represented the South Derbyshire District XI.

Price, Steve 'Asda' (as in Asda price) formed a formidable bowling partnership with Frazer Harrison. Asda's appeals can be heard throughout the county! Played in the 2010 Harry Lund Cup Final and is now the club's kit supplier through his sports shop - Cricket Box. Took 54 wickets in the 1995 season with a best bowling of 6 for 35 at an average of 12.33. In 2006 won the most improved player trophy; he had only been playing for

20 years at that point! He played in the 1st XI that gained successive promotions in the early 2000s. Unfortunately for Steve, he is also remembered as being the only Melbourne senior cricketer to be bowled, when playing against Derby Congs, by a member of the opposite sex. He claims it was a pea roller that crept under his bat. The biggest grins didn't belong to the umpire, the other team or bowler, but his so-called team mates.

Rafferty, Dominic A good cricketer and clubman. He played in the 1st XI that gained successive promotions in the early 2000s.

Rafferty, P Played in the 1993 season, averaging 25.55 runs with a high score of 61.

Randon, C In the Derby Mercury report of August 18th 1875 he is listed as the club professional playing against a Derby XI. He bowled 9 overs, 3 maidens and took 6 wickets for 9 runs. Of the wickets, 4 were bowled and 3 caught and bowled.

Reading, A Played in the early 1990s; topped the bowling averages in 1990.

Rees, J Played in the 1992 season; highest score of 15 and took 4 wickets.

Reeve, Emma Girlfriend of one of the players and scorer/tea lady for the 1st XI in 1999.

Richards, L Played in the late 1990s; a good all-rounder who took 34 wickets in the 1996 season with a best of 6 for 58. In 1998, topped the batting averages with 240 runs at an average of 60.

Rippin, Lee First played in 1998, averaging 20.5 that season.

Robey, Richard Played in the 1960s before going on to play for Ticknall for many years. A very good wicketkeeper and batsman who has run the Liberal Club in Melbourne for many years.

Robinson, J Played in the team that reopened the cricket facilities on May 12th 1951 after the club and ground had closed down during World War 2.

Robinson, N Local player from the mid 1980s.

Robson, S Played against Ashby on July 20th 1890 and scored 3 runs.

Rolfs, Simon A rugby player and tri-athlete, he is a very capable cricketing all-rounder. Played in the 2010 Harry Lund Cup Final.

Roome, Amy Girlfriend of one of the players and scorer/tea lady for the 1st XI in 1999.

Rossi, Mark Judged by many to be one of the best batsmen to have played for the club. Played for rivals Ticknall as a youngster, as did his father. A regular 500 runs a season player who has stayed loyal to the club even though his talent could have taken him elsewhere. Still has many years of cricketing to come. Played in the 1st XI that gained successive promotions in the early 2000s.

Rost, Bruno   A good batsman who played for several seasons; son of the former MP for South Derbyshire, Peter Rost. Currently playing for Brailsford.

Rutherford, A   Local player from the mid 1980s.

Salisbury, T   Played against Woodville on May 20th 1896 and scored 2 not out.

Salsbury, Jas W   Captain of the 1st XI in 1920.

Salsbury, M E   Captain of the 1912 Derby and District League Championship team.

Salt, Richard   Played in 2005.

Sargent, R   Played in the 1993 season.

Saunders, Matt   A cricketer and footballer of great promise whose life was cut tragically short. He played for the club between 1992 and 1999. The club score box was built in his memory in 2004 by parents Mick and Janet.

Saxby, N   Player from the 1960s.

Scott, Lee   Played in 2005.

Sellars, Mr   Played against Messrs Allsopp and company on July 29th 1874 and scored 6 runs.

Sharma, Parwan   Played in 2008.

Sharma, Ravi   Played in 2008.

Shaw, Gerry   Played in the team that reopened the cricket facilities on May 12th 1951 after the club and ground had closed down during World War 2. Captained the 2nd XI in 1939.

Sheldon, K   Local player from the late 1970s and early 1980s.

Sherwin, C   Played against Alvaston on September 15th 1869 and scored 6 runs.

Shields, J   Played against Kegworth in 1900 and scored 3 not out.

Short, K   Played in 1990; batting average of 15.52.

Singh, Aranjit   All-rounder who made his debut in 2010.

Singleton, W   Played against Draycott on May 31st 1893 and scored 11 runs.

Slater, Alex   Current 1st XI Captain and club Secretary who has almost single-handedly organised the playing side of the club for several years. An authentic all-rounder who can keep wicket. He also plays football and tennis for Melbourne and has continued the family tradition working in the

Welcome Cafe. Batting average of 46.0 and high score of 152 in the 1995 season. Captained the 1st XI when they gained successive promotions in the early 2000s.

Slater, Jo   The mother of Alex and Matt, who supplies great teas to both teams and does the catering at the popular Welcome Cafe in Melbourne.

Slater, Matt   Brother of Alex and a very good all-round cricketer who played in the 2010 Legends game. In the 2001 season, averaged 19.5 with the bat, with a high score of 45 not out. Played in the 1st XI that gained successive promotions in the early 2000s.

Smart, Steve   A local player from the mid 1980s; a good and loyal clubman. Brother-in-law of Robert Marshall.

Smith, F   Captain of the 2nd XI in 1929.

Smith, G   A player from the very early days of the club, who appeared in the 1860s.

Smith, H D   Played against Alvaston on September 15th 1869 and scored 1 run but took 4 wickets.

Smith, J   Player from the mid 1950s.

Smith, J D   Played against Kegworth in the 1900 season.

Smith, James   Jimbo was the 2nd XI Captain between 2009 and 2010, who captained the side in the 2010 Harry Lund Cup Final and when they gained promotion in 2009. A good clubman who always gives 100% for the club and team.

Smith, T   Played against Alvaston on September 15th 1869 and scored 5 runs.

Smithson, Colin   An unassuming cricketer who plays and approaches the game with a gentlemanly outlook. In the 1991 season, averaged 19.44 with the bat, with a high score of 49 not out for the 2nd XI.

Spare, Brian   Brother of Frank and a highly rated local sports manager who managed local football teams including Breedon, Melbourne and Gresley Rovers. Umpired for MTCC in the 1970s and was Fixture Secretary for many years.

Spare, Frank   Player from the 1960s who lived at Stanton by Bridge. Brother of Brian.

Spare, Fred   Brother of Malcom and an enthusisastic cricketer who played in the 1960s.

Spare, Malcom   Brother of Fred and an excellent bowler and batsman in the 1960s and 1970s, who served with distinction in the Derbyshire police force. Always likely to hit runs and take wickets. He was highly respected by the young players of the time, particularly the author of this book.

Stanhope, Phil   Slow right arm bowler who played for the 2nd XI for one year in 2009 and took a very impressive total of 98 wickets in all games that season.

Staniforth, Alan   All-rounder from the 1950s and 1960s who played in the 1965 Butterley Cup Final. He still lives in Melbourne and was Captain of the 2nd XI in the 1960s.

Stanley, Andy   Good left-handed opening batsman who made his maiden century in 2010 against Alvaston and Boulton. As a youngster, he played for Nottingham Boys.

Stanwix, N   Played in the early 1990s; batting average of 21.67 with a high score of 65 in 1993.

Starkie, Jenny   Wife of Mike who is the club's welfare officer. She has always been a part of the club's fundraising efforts, in addition to making the teas.

Starkie, Mike   Mike has played for the club since moving to the area in the 1970s. Although not as mobile as in his heyday, he can still make runs with grace and style. Still good enough to score 85 against Castle Donington in 2007. He has also served the club well off the field and has been a Chairman of the club.

Statham, S   A player from the very early days of the club who appeared in the 1860s.

Statham, T   A player from the very early days of the club who appeared in the 1860s.

Stockley, B   Player from the mid 1990s.

Stone, E   Won the best bowling award for the 2nd XI in 1896.

Stone, Mrs   Tea lady from the 1970s and 1980s.

Stringer, J   Played for the 2nd XI in 2005; high score of 26 that season.

Sumner, J   Player from the 1960s.

Swallow, Elaine   Wife of Mark, supplier of super teas, as you would expect, from the wife of the local cricket tea critic.

Swallow, Mark   A dedicated clubman who, he will readily admit, is not the best player but fields with enthusiasm and is a very dependable taker of catches using the 'claw' method. Current Chairman of the Tail End Club and enthusiastic grader of the away cricket teas. Never mind the quality of the opposition, what's the quality of the teas? Do not leave anything on the side of the plate, expecting it to be there when you return.

Swallow, Paul   Son of Mark and a very good footballer and cricketer. Won the 2nd XI fielding trophy in 2007.

Swarbrook, W Local player from the late 1970s and early 1980s who opened the bowling. Took 5 wickets against Hilton on May 5th 1979.

Sylvester, Adrian Brother of Dean, who played in the 1970s and 1980s. A good local footballer.

Sylvester, Dean Brother of Adrian, who played in the 1970s and 1980s. A good rugby player.

Talbot, B Played in the early 1990s.

Tate, M Player from the 1960s.

Taylor, Sam Moved to the club from Kirk Langley in 2010. An excellent fielder. Played in the 2010 Harry Lund Cup Final.

Taylor, Steve Local player from the late 1970s and early 1980s.

Thornton, James Player from the late 1990s; batting average of 69.75 with a high score of 129 not out in the 2000 season. Played in the 1st XI that gained successive promotions in the early 2000s.

Thornton, N Player from the mid 1990s with a batting average of 40.3 and a high score of 91 not out in 1995.

Tidman, A Player from the mid 1950s.

Tivey, E A member of the 1912 Derby and District League Championship team.

Tivey, F C A member of the 1912 Derby and District League Championship team.

Tivey, Leon Captain of the 1st XI in 1956; also captained the 2nd XI in 1952. Took 5 wickets for 12 runs against Draycott on June 11th 1955.

Tivey, Richard Fast-bowler of the late 1960s and 1970s. On his day, extremely fast and capable of taking many wickets. A long memory, particularly when recalling who had bowled him a short ball in previous seasons. He also kept goal for Melbourne Town Football Club.

Tivey, S E A member of the 1912 Derby and District League Championship team.

Tivey, Steve Player from the 1980s. Scored 46 not out against Borrowash on June 3rd 1984 and took 4 wickets for 22 runs in the same match.

Tivey, W Player from the mid 1950s.

Tomlin, Ivan Honorary Secretary in 1929, in succession to the legendary J F Andrews.

Tomlinson, David Son of Derek who played for the club in the 1970s.

Tomlinson, Derek Batsman and wicketkeeper from Little Eaton who played in the 1960s.

Toon, Charles 'Bud' was rated as one of the best opening pace bowlers in the district and operated in tandem with Vic Jackson. First played in 1954 and for many years afterwards.

Topliss, Colin Local player from the early 1980s.
Tranmer, Wayne All-rounder from the early 1980s.
Turner, Chris Moved into the area from the south. A keen and energetic cricketer who will always do his best for the club.

c 1963
Harold Hodgkinson with (left to right) Brenda Bentley (Parnham),
Lynn Bentley, Jean Bentley and Mrs Turner. (51)

Turner, John 1st XI Captain in 1966, taking over from Fred Bentley. A very dependable slow bowler and batsman who approached the game with great seriousness. Also captained the 2nd XI in 1964. First played in the mid 1950s and took 5 wickets for 30 runs against Ockbrook and Borrowash on May 14th 1955.
Turner, Mrs To most players she was only known as Mrs Turner, mother of John and our regular tea lady in the 1960s and 70s. She was also head of the Sunday school at Melbourne Church.
Twells, Graham Played for the 2nd XI in the 1970s and early 1980s. A good batsman who still lives in Melbourne.
Underwood, F Played against Worthington and company on August 3rd 1870 and scored 14 runs.

Wakefield, Andy 'Ringo' was a young player from the early 1980s who still lives in nearby Breedon. A good footballer who now devotes his leisure time to playing golf. Brother of Phillip and cousin of Colin.

Wakefield, Colin 'Wakie' has lived in neighbouring Breedon, man and boy, and played as a youngster for what was then the premier village team in the East Midlands (as did many of his family), but then came to play for Melbourne. Has been playing for the club for over 40 years and by most accounts has taken well over 1,000 wickets for the club during that time. Still more than capable of bowling a side out. Played in the Harry Lund Cup Final in 2010. Now more known as a bowler, but an accomplished batsman over the years. Captained the 1st XI in 1981. Played in the 1st XI that gained successive promotions in the early 2000s.

Wakefield, Phillip Player from the late 1970s who took 4 wickets for 21 runs against Muggington on May 19th 1979. Brother of Andy and cousin of Colin.

Walker, A Player from the mid 1950s.

Walker, G Player from the 1960s.

Walker, Terry Played in the late 1990s.

Walker, Tony Played in the late 1990s.

Ward, Jack Played in 2006 and 2007; current defender with the Melbourne Dynamos FC.

Ward, Melville 2nd XI scorer in 1908.

Watkins, N Local player from the early 1980s.

Webster, F 1st XI umpire in 1932.

Weightman, Martin Played in 2009 in the Loughborough League.

Weston, M Player from the 1960s.

Whyatt, Graham Graham played in the 1960s and was a sound batsman and fielder, who was always a popular member of the team.

Whyatt, Peter Left arm fast-bowler of the 1960s who played in the 1965 Butterley cup final.

Wilcox, M Player from the 1960s.

Wild, Paul Current player and swing bowler.

Wildsmith, F Played against Alvaston on Sep, 15th 1869. Out for a duck.

Wileman, Tony Tosh was a good all-rounder who came over from Breedon with Richard North and Aubrey Gadsby and played for the 2nd XI in the late 1960s.

Wilkinson, S Player from the 1960s and also played local football for Breedon, still involved in cricket working at the indoor net facility at the County ground in Derby.

Williams, C Played in the 1992 season with a batting average of 11.6 and a high score of 56.

Williamson, C Player from the 1960s.

Williamson, R Player from the 1960s.

Wilson, Doug Player from the 1960s.

Wilson, Eric Umpire for the club in the 1960s and 1970s. Always accompanied by his dog Rusty.

Wilson, Guy Dennis See Ch 11 - Melbourne Players Who Played First Class Cricket.

Wilson, J A member of the 1912 Derby and District League Championship team and Captain in 1905. Also made 53 runs playing against a Mr Wells XI in 1893.

Wilson, W Player from the 1960s.

Winters, F Player from the mid 1950s.

Winters, Mark Played as a youngster and went on to become one of the best batsmen to have made runs for the club. Was one of the youngest Captains of the club and a natural leader. A good all-round sportsman who played in the Legends game in 2010. Scored 106 not out against Sudbury on July 15th 1979.

Winters, Paul Brother of Mark; a good cricketer and golfer who played in the late 1980s.

Wood, Albert The club's current 1st XI scorer.

Wood, P Played in the 1993 season.

Woodburn, Dave Played for the club in the mid 1980s.

Woodburn, J Player from the 1980s, who scored 55 against Pastures on July 3rd 1984.

Woodward, K Local player from the late 1970s and early 1980s. Played in the match against Derby Congs when Melbourne were 6 all out.

Woolley, Dave Played in 2009 in the Loughborough League.

Wooton, J Played against Ashby on September 10th 1862, scoring 19 runs and taking one catch.

Wright, A Player from the 1960s.

Wright, L A batting average of 11 in the 1895 season.

Wright, M Local player from the late 1970s and early 1980s.

Yasin, Tariq Played in the 1992 season with a highest score of 20.

Young, John Henry See Ch 11 - Melbourne Players Who Played First Class Cricket.

Young, W Achieved a batting average of 6.5 in the 1895 season and also took 13 wickets. A possible relative of J H Young.

APPENDICES

"Display high standards of behaviour"

Club Playing Development Plan 2011 - 2013

The Club's Vision

Develop members to their maximum potential, playing at the highest level they can achieve within a community based club.

The Club's Aims

- Provide structured training and coaching for all members.

- Develop club players from the junior system into players for the senior teams.

- Provide facilities for the sporting and social needs of the club.

- Provide facilities to the required standards of the league, meeting the needs of the club.

- Ensure the management, organisation and administration meets the requirements of the English Cricket Board and Derbyshire Cricket Board.

- Create an ethos and atmosphere that engages the whole club, gives support for all teams and encourages greater volunteer involvement.

- Improve promotion of the club to members, sponsors and the local community.

- Ensure financial growth meets development plans.

The Sporting Partnership

The club is a member of the Melbourne Sporting Partnership which is currently working alongside the South Derbyshire County Council to review and develop the sports and social facilities at the ground. The group hopes that, within four years, the ground and facilities will be transformed into a modern amenity that will service the sports needs of Melbourne for generations to come.

Chaired by County and District Councillor John Harrison (former Melbourne cricketer), the partnership consists of representatives from the sports clubs of Melbourne including cricket, football, rugby, bowls and tennis. Representatives from the SDDC's Leisure and Recreation group are also in attendance at meetings.

The plans include:

- A new pavilion, servicing the needs of all the clubs currently using the ground. It will include changing facilities, social facilities, storage and a balcony overlooking the playing areas.

- New drainage of all pitches.

- The levelling of the old rugby pitch.

- New tennis courts.

- New flat bowling green.

- A new running trail.

- A new children's playground.

- A second cricket square with artificial wicket.

Codes of Conduct

Melbourne Town Cricket Club is fully committed to safeguarding and promoting the wellbeing of all its members. The Club believes it is important that officials, players, members, coaches, administrators and parents associated with the club should, at all times, show respect and understanding for the safety and welfare of others.

All members and guests of Melbourne Town Cricket Club will:

- Respect the rights, dignity and worth of every person within the context of Cricket.

- Treat everyone equally and not discriminate on the grounds of age, gender, disability, race, ethnic origin, nationality, colour, parental or marital status, religious belief, class or social background, sexual preference or political belief.

- Not condone, or allow to go unchallenged, any form of discrimination if witnessed.

- Display high standards of behaviour.

- Promote the positive aspects of Cricket e.g. fair play.

- Encourage all participants to learn the laws and rules and play within them, respecting the decisions of match officials.

- Actively discourage unfair play, rule violations and arguments with match officials.

- Recognise and reward good performances, not just match results.

- Place the wellbeing and safety of young people above the development of performance.

- Ensure that activities are appropriate for the age, maturity, experience and ability of the individual.

- Respect young people's opinions when making decisions about their participation in Cricket.

- Not smoke, drink or use banned substances whilst actively working with young people in the club.

- Not provide young people with alcohol when they are under the care of the club.

- Follow ECB guidelines set out in the 'Safe Hands – Cricket's Policy for Safeguarding Children' and any other relevant guidelines issued.

- Report any concerns in relation to a young person, following reporting procedures laid down by the ECB.

In addition to Codes of Conduct, all Club Officers and Appointed Volunteers will:

- Hold relevant qualifications and be covered by appropriate insurance.

- Always work in an open environment (i.e. avoid private or unobserved situations and encourage an open environment).

- Inform players and parents of the requirements of Cricket.

- Know and understand the ECB's 'Safe Hands – Cricket's Policy for Safeguarding Children'.

Members Policy for Juniors

Melbourne Town Cricket Club is fully committed to
safeguarding and promoting the wellbeing of all its members.

Members are encouraged to be open at all times and to share any
concerns or complaints that they may have about any aspect of the club
with the club chairman and the officers of the club.

As members of Melbourne Town Cricket Club, juniors are expected
to abide by the following junior code of conduct:

1. All members must play within the rules and respect officials and
    their decisions.

2. All members must respect the rights, dignity and worth of all
    participants regardless of gender, ability, cultural background or
    religion.

3. Members should keep to agreed timings for training and
    competitions or inform their coach or team manager if they are
    going to be late.

4. Members must wear suitable kit for training and match sessions,
    as agreed with the Captain/coach/team manager.

5. Members must pay promptly any fees for training or events.

6. Junior members are not allowed to smoke on club premises or
    whilst representing the club at competitions.

7. Junior members are not allowed to consume alcohol or drugs of
    any kind on the club premises or whilst representing the club.

Club Officials

Patron: Lord Ralph Kerr
President: Mr G R Heath
Vice Presidents: L Barber, D Bellis, D Calvert, R Crossley, R Grummett,
C F Heafield, F Heafield, J Roberts, T Potts, C Toon
Chairman: T Potts
Vice Chairman: C Wakefield
Honorary Club and Fixture Secretary: A Slater
Honorary Treasurer: Mrs S Potts
Auditor: J Hallifield
Welfare Officer: Mrs J Starkie
Committee Members: V Hallifield, C Lancaster, S Price, M Swallow

Club Coach (ECB Level 2): J Humpidge
Club Coaches (ECB Level 1): P Fletcher, K Grant, A Heafield,
J Jenkinson, J Lacey, D Marshall
Head Groundsman: K Grant
Club Umpire: N Bowes
Captains: 1st XI A Slater, 2nd XI K Grant, Development XI A Heafield
Vice Captains: 1st XI M Rossi, 2nd XI Andy Stanley
Indoor Cricket Captain: V Hallifield
Kwik Cricket: D Fletcher, J Jenkinson, Mrs S Potts
Under 13s Team Managers: J Lacey, D Marshall,
Club Scorers: 1st XI A Wood; 2nd XI Miss H Burton
Publicity: A Heafield

Web Site: D Marshall
Melbourne Sporting Partnership Representative: M Starkie
Sponsorship: A Slater. Telephone 07966 933583

Club Development Manager: A Heafield
Telephone 01332 865422, 07722 485213, e mail to
a.heafield@btinternet.com

150TH Anniversary Celebrations

This book is a part of the 150th anniversary celebrations and during the year 2011 many celebratory events are being planned. These include a Race Night, Promises Auction and a Black Tie Dinner. However, for cricketing purists it is the visit of the Marylebone Cricket Club that will cause the most excitement.

The world famous MCC is bringing a team to play the MTCC in late July. This will be a day match starting at 11.30am and a team will be selected to represent the MTCC in this very prestigious fixture. The MCC, as it is universally known, was founded in 1787 as a private members' club, dedicated to the development of cricket. It owns, and is based at, Lord's Cricket Ground near St John's Wood in north London. The MCC was formerly the governing body of cricket in England and across the world. The club has 18,000 full members and 4,000 associate members. Members have special rights to use the pavilion and other stands at Lord's for all matches played at the ground.

The red and gold colours of the MCC are famous through the world of cricket; current Honorary Life Members of the club include Sir Garfield Sobers, Sunil Gavaskar, Alec Stewart, Rachael Heyhoe-Flint, Shane Warne, Glenn McGrath, Michael Vaughan and Graeme Hick. Music lyricist, Sir Tim Rice, is a trustee of the club.

On hearing the news, Melbourne Club Chairman, Tel Potts, said:
"This a great honour for the club and Melbourne. We will give our honoured guests a day, and game, to remember and we hope that the town will turn out in force to see this unique match."

At a time of great upheaval for cricket, the MCC has for many people come to represent a citadel for tradition against the ever-changing landscape of the modern game. Although the MCC plays over 500 matches in this country and overseas, it doesn't play against club teams that often.

The match against the MCC, uniquely, in this day of limited overs matches, will be an all day match starting at 11.30am and is taking place on Sunday, July 31st. The MCC team will be announced nearer the date but it will include a sprinkling of former county cricket players, bolstered by some of the top young cricketers in the Midlands.

The biggest problem will be who to select to represent the club. To play for Melbourne in a match against the MCC is a once in a lifetime opportunity and it is hoped that all players will make themselves available. Whilst we want to put out a team that is representative of a community based club like ours, we also want to win. What village cricketer wouldn't want on his cricket CV, "played against the MCC"?

150 years of Melbourne Cricket

The MTCC 150th anniversary tie in club blue and yellow with the MTCC motif and 150 years of Melbourne Cricket is available.

Contact Andy Heafield on 01332 865422

Price £14.99 plus postage and packing

The club would like to thank the Derbyshire County Council Cultural and Community Services for their assistance in the production of this book.

Bibliography

The following have either been quoted or useful in the research of this book:

'D W Jardine Spartan Cricketer' by C Douglas
'W G's Birthday Party' by D Knyaston
'Pavilions in the Park', a history of Melbourne Cricket Club by A Batchelder
'How You Played the Game', A life of Grantland Rice by William A Harper
'Groucho and Me', the Autobiography by Groucho Marx
'A Last English Summer' by Duncan Hamilton
'The Spirit of Cricket' by Colin Cowdrey and Ted Dexter
'When An Old Cricketer Leaves The Crease' by Roy Harper, 1975.

The following web sites have provided information as background to the research of this book:

http://melbourne.play-cricket.com/home/home.asp
http:/ancestry.co.uk
http://www.melbournevillagevoice.co.uk
http://dpcl.play-cricket.com/home/home.asp
http://www.cricketpoetry.com/Videos.aspx
http://www.ticknall.org.uk
http://www.benefice.org.uk
http://www.melbourne-uk.com
http://www.mhrg.org.uk - the web site of the Melbourne Historical Research Group
http://www.mcc.org.au - the web site of Melbourne Cricket Club, Australia
http://www.lords.org/mcc/about-mcc - the web site of the Marylebone CC
http://cricketarchive.com
http://en.wikipedia.org/wiki/Lord_Walter_Kerr

The archives of the Derby Mercury can be accessed through the website of the Derbyshire County Council libraries service:
http://www.derbyshire.gov.uk/leisure/libraries/online
And lastly, where would any research be without wikipedia and wikiHow? The Art of Melbourne Captaincy is based on a list that first appeared in wikiHow?

Photographs and Illustrations

The photos for this book have been kindly provided by:

Fig	Page	Acknowledgment	Fig	Page	Acknowledgment
1	6	Melbourne Hall	27	51	Steve Price
2	7	M T C C	28	53	Andy Heafield
3	8	M T C C	29	57	John Harrison
4	13	Jayne Wright	30	58	Melbourne Hall
5	16	Colin Wakefield	31	60	Keith Foster
6	20	Gail Potts	32	63	Gail Potts
7	22	Gail Potts	33	64	Richard Hatton collection
8	31	Richard Heath	34	65	Richard Hatton collection
9	33	Richard Hatton collection	35	69	Andy Heafield
10	34	Richard Hatton collection	36	70	Len Hall
11	35	Richard Hatton collection	37	72	Len Hall
12	36	Richard Hatton collection	38	73	Len Hall
13	36	Richard Hatton collection	39	74	Len Hall
14	37	Richard Hatton collection	40	76	Len Hall
15	38	Richard Hatton collection	41	80	Bob Chambers
16	39	Richard Hatton collection	42	88	Richard Hatton collection
17	40	Richard Hatton collection	43	94	Robert Marshall
18	40	Richard Hatton collection	44	97	Richard Hatton collection
19	41	Richard Hatton collection	45	101	Gail Potts
20	42	Richard Hatton collection	46	104	Richard Hatton collection
21	43	Richard Hatton collection	47	106	Melbourne Civic Society
22	44	Richard Hatton collection	48	115	Richard Hatton collection
23	45	Melbourne Civic Society	49	117	Richard Hatton collection
24	46	Melbourne Civic Society	50	118	Len Hall
25	48	Richard Hatton collection	51	129	Richard Hatton collection
26	49	Richard Hatton collection	52	143	Fred Heafield

I am indebted to Jayne Wright for allowing me to use one of her watercolours. There are more paintings on her web site www.jaynewright.com

Acknowledgements

"I see them as they were then: youthful, full of vigour"

This book couldn't have been compiled without the assistance, memories and photographs of:

Bernard Baines of Derby Congs, Lennie Barber, David Bellis, Alan Bradley, The Bygones section of the Derby Telegraph, David Calvert, Keith Foster, Robert Gent and the Derbyshire County Council Cultural and Community Services, John Hallifield, George Harris, County and District Councillor John Harrison, the late Richard Hatton, Carolyn Hazlehurst (née Hatton), Frank Heafield, Fred Heafield, Rodney Heafield, Philip Heath, Richard Heath, Alan Hicklin, Lord Ralph Kerr, Graham Leach, The Magic Attic Archives (Swadlincote), Robert Marshall, The Melbourne Civic Society, The Melbourne Historical Research Group, Tel Potts, Sarah Poulson, Malcom Spare, the late Brian Spare, Ian Turner, Village Voice (Melbourne and District), Gill Weston - the Curator at Melbourne Hall, Colin Wakefield.

The help of Len Hall, the grandson of Jim Horsley, was invaluable and my thanks go to him for allowing me access to his grandfather's fascinating cricketing memorabilia. I only wish that cameras had been around to record Big Jim's hat trick and twelve match wickets against the touring Australians in 1919.

Jean Grimley has done a sterling job of proof reading the book. Thank you.

I have listed as many former players and contributors to the club as can be remembered in the directory, but there will no doubt be someone who has been omitted. My apologies to anyone I may have forgotten in all of the above.

Author's Note

Most young boys when growing up have sporting heroes. I was no different: however many of the sports stars I looked up to weren't to be seen on the international stage; they usually appeared at the cricket ground in Melbourne. Maybe it was because they were more accessible, but Malcom Spare, Fred Bentley, Bas Farmer, Tel Potts and several others were the men of the moment for me. When I got older and actually appeared in the same team as some of them, I still held them in great respect. Even now when I meet the ones that are still with us, I see them as they were then: youthful, full of vigour and about to take wickets or launch mighty sixes over the boundary. Without them, and all the other Melbourne players, this book and the memories it contains would not exist and, for those players not with us any longer, wherever you are, may the wicket be good, the umpires impartial and the competition fair.

A final thanks to my father Fred, my earliest cricketing hero.

Andy Heafield, April 2011

The author
10 years old, practising in his back garden.
He still can't get the hang of this batting lark.
(52)